JUST CALL ME

soldier boy

World War II Letters
from Pfc. Andy Bergner, Patton's Third Army
Edited by Laurie Bergner Maggiano
Historical research by Ronald C. Maggiano

Windsor Publishing

Printed in the United States of America.

First Edition: July 2013

ISBN 978-0615844817

For Audrey

JUST CALL ME SOLDIER BOY

PROLOGUE

Private Andy Bergner with his German shepherd, Don.

My father never talked about the war. When, as young children, we asked if he had been a soldier, if he fought in a war, he would say with quiet pride that he served in Patton's Third Army during World War II, but then he would quickly divert our attention. This was not especially hard to do. There were five of us, two girls and three boys, living with our parents, Audrey and Andrew Bergner, in a wonderfully funky old house near Valley Forge, Pennsylvania, and we were easily amused.

Then one day the boys found the knives buried in Aunt Matilda, our name for the old trunk that our great grandmother brought with her when she emigrated from Germany. Excitement reigned in the attic. There was a U.S. army dagger in its green woven sheath, just like the kind our G.I. Joe doll carried on his belt. There were two fierce looking knives with elegant scroll work and foreign writing on the blades and carved hilts with silver inlay. "Did you stab anybody with these knives? Did you steal them from dead Germans? Did you have a gun? How many Germans did you shoot? Did you kill anybody?"

Our questions were urgent, yet even in the face of this seemingly immutable evidence, Dad said little. The trench knife, he explained, was a standard issue side arm that he used mostly for opening K - Rations and letters from home. The other knives he bought from some German soldiers after the war ended. They were souvenirs, gifts for his father, our Pop Pop Bergner, who would appreciate the workmanship. What a letdown for the boys - no blood, no guts, just souvenirs.

As we grew up and took our respective American and European history courses, Dad would engage in discussions of the war, its causes, strategies, outcomes, the Marshall Plan, etc., but there was never talk about his war experience. He had one or two funny stories that he would repeat when pressed, like the time his platoon "liberated" a German underwear factory after several weeks without a change of clothes - only to be disappointed to discover that it only produced ladies panties - or the time after VE Day when he challenged a Russian soldier to a marksmanship contest and won a fancy Russian wrist watch. He did tell us how lucky he was that the Army assigned him to mess duty at Fort McClellan in Alabama after the war. He would laugh and tell us again that when he married our Mom all she knew how to cook were brownies and chocolate chip cookies. If the Army hadn't taught him to cook, they would have starved!

After World War II ended there were insufficient jobs for the hundreds of thousands of G.I.s returning home, so the government kept many soldiers in stateside service for up to two years after the final armistice. G.I.s were released from service based on a point system with points earned for duration of service, overseas duty, battles, medals and other factors. Dad didn't have enough points to earn release when he returned from Europe and spent another year as a peacetime soldier, scrambling eggs and peeling vegetables.

Dad was also grateful to Uncle Sam for sending him to Villanova University on the G.I. Bill where he earned a bachelor's degree in mechanical engineering. He later earned a master's degree in engineering management from Hofstra University in New York (though my mother always claimed credit for that degree since she transcribed all of Dad's study notes into a master's thesis). Dad and his older brother Joe went to Villanova together. The G.I. Bill paid tuition (then $500 a semester including books and lab fees) and provided a $75 per month living allowance. They turned $40 of this stipend over to my Gran Mom Bergner since they were living at home, keeping the balance for gas and clothes. For extra spending money they had a business simonizing cars at $5 per car. They shined four cars per weekend, which in 1947 was enough for dates.

And that was it. To us, Dad's war experience, such as it was, consisted of liberating ladies underwear, cooking eggs for 200 G.I.s and going to college. There were no stories of combat, fear, excitement, agony or ecstasy. It was pretty boring, so as kids we stopped asking questions and that suited Dad just fine.

That changed in 1995.

On the 50th anniversary of VE Day, May 8, 1995, my parents came to our home for a family dinner and Dad brought along a thick, three - ringed binder. It was old, covered in a blue denim fabric and decorated on the front with foil American flags. Inside were 270 letters written by my father between September 1944, when he was inducted into the U.S. Army two months after his 18th birthday, and July 1946, the month he was deactivated to attend Villanova.

This is a collection of contemporaneous World War II letters, written by the young boy who grew up to be my father. As an historian and history teacher who well knows the value of primary source documents, my husband Ron was awestruck that such a record existed in our family. To me, it was staggering that I was seeing this binder for the first time when I was a grown woman with my own teenage children. Where was this document when we were kids? How did my father keep it hidden? How come we didn't find it?

Dad's engineering degrees propelled him into the nascent aerospace program where he contributed to the Gemini, Mercury, Saturn and Apollo launches while working for General Electric Corporation. During his 20 years with G.E. we moved - a lot - tracking rockets around the country. From Valley Forge we moved to the Jet Propulsion Laboratory in California, back to Pennsylvania, down to Cape Kennedy in Florida and eventually west to Arizona. Between job transfers and my mother's desire for the next, best house, we moved seven times between my sixth and 16th birthdays. Packing, unpacking, weeding out what wasn't needed or too expensive to ship was one of my duties as the eldest daughter. I swore I knew the contents of every box in our attic– but I had never seen this binder. Reading the letters, hearing for the first time, in his own 18-year-old voice what he was thinking and feeling as he prepared for and served in a bloody war, gave me a new perspective on and respect for this dear, quiet man.

My father was among the last wave of young Americans to be drafted to the war. He arrived in Europe just after the Bulge but just in time for the final push by Patton's Third Army into Germany, across the Rhine, to meet the Russian Red Guard at Chemnitz and pinch off Hitler forever. He spent only six months overseas. His service was short but brutal. He was never wounded and didn't earn a purple heart. His prize was coming home alive.

The power of these letters is not in their sensationalism - the censors would have stricken any references to battle positions or action. Nor is this a tale of the type of heroism that sells tickets at the box office. Yet in reading these funny, homey, pious, sometimes painful letters, a hero emerges who speaks through these documents on behalf of hundreds of thousands of 18-year-old heroes who left the Boy Scouts and baseball fields and paper routes of middle class America for the killing fields of war. This is a coming-of-age story. The story of a boy who had not yet started to shave before being shipped out to reinforce the exhausted troops in France and Germany. It is the story of a boy confronting issues of patriotism, faith and honor to become the man he is today, a man who when at age 85 was asked to represent World War II veterans in a Fourth of July parade, would only agree to do so if he could carry a sign that read, "War is a Last Resort".

Andy Bergner was raised in a close-knit German/American community in North East Philadelphia. A product of Catholic schools, his life revolved around family, church and odd jobs in his grandfather's candy store. He was sweet and funny and eager and his nickname, Gump, somehow suited him. In 1944, only three months after graduation from North East Catholic High School, Andy was "selected" to join the United States Army.

PROLOGUE

In October he reported to Camp Joseph T. Robinson in Little Rock, Arkansas, for basic training. Here he encountered for the first time boys from outside his parochial world, boys that swore, drank, smoked, played poker and didn't go to church. He was scandalized. Having passed my own teen years in the halcyon 1960s and early 70s, this image of my naïve, sincere father was both surprising and sweet. He must have adapted though because he became a great poker player during boot camp, a pastime he would enjoy all his life.

Due to the urgent need for infantry in Europe in the weeks leading up to the final push into Germany, Dad's 17 weeks of basic training were cut to 13. With other newly minted soldiers, still very green, he was given a 10-day furlough to say his goodbyes to family before crossing to Scotland on the British troop ship, *Aquitania*, in February 1945. By March he was in the midst of battle and in May 1945, after two months of short but brutal action in France and Germany, victory was declared in Europe. But VE Day didn't bring an end to Andy's war in Europe. He soon joined the occupation force, all the while hoping and praying he would not be re-deployed to Japan. Finally, there was that wonderful day in August 1945 when he left Southampton, headed for home, expecting to arrive, as he described it, in three S's - Safe, Sound and Soon.

This is the story of Andy's war, but we would not have this historical record were it not for Mary Jane Waterman. Miss Waterman was, in the parlance of her time, a spinster lady who at age 35 still lived with her mother. In 1944 the pair moved into the house next door to my father's family home on Rising Sun Avenue in Philadelphia. Dad says Mary Jane was very attractive, a tall brunette who had a good job as personal secretary to the president and vice president of Quaker City Rubber Company. There was some curiosity about why such a good looking and vivacious lady remained unmarried, but folks were more respectful of privacy in those days and Mary Jane kept her own counsel. Mama Waterman and "MJ" soon became great friends of the Bergners, sharing meals and exchanging baked goods and home grown produce. Dad thought she was a swell neighbor especially after she got him a temporary job at the loading dock of Quaker City Rubber Company the summer before he reported for basic training. MJ drove Dad to the plant each day and they became friends. When Dad left for the service MJ promised to write to him. And write she did.

In the almost two years Dad was in the Army, Mary Jane wrote him more than 450 letters. These were not letters from a sweetheart; they were big sister letters - letters that brought him news from home, letters that cheered or encouraged or gently chastised him. To break the monotony she wrote on all different types of paper, oversized sheets, scrolls, desk blotters and, once, paper toweling from the company washroom. She also sent regular packages full of food stuffs, cakes baked by her mother or my grandmother, photographs, magazines, ink and paper, pen knives, a camera and other items he asked for. And weekly, without fail, Mary Jane sent a box of peanuts in the shell, the kind you get at baseball games, for which she was nicknamed "Peanut" by all of Dad's G.I. buddies. What I found most amazing, though, is that Mary Jane did not just carry on this correspondence and gifting with my father. She wrote regularly to several other G.I.s including Dad's older brothers - Joe, serving stateside in the Marines, and Fritz, a civilian contractor to the Army Air Corps in the Philippines. Dad is sure he was her favorite, however. One wonders if each boy she wrote to felt that way.

In any war, most attention is quite rightly focused on the men and women who are in armed service, yet there are many ways to serve. Mary Jane Waterman served her country well by writing letters to scared young G.I.s, including Andrew L. Bergner, Private 1st Class, L Company, 417th Regiment, 76th Infantry, "Old Blood and Guts" Third Army. I am ever grateful for her service. Only a few of Mary Jane's letters to my father were preserved. But the great gift she gave to my family was to save, in a blue denim binder decorated with foil flags, all the letters Dad wrote to her, letters that somehow would stay hidden from the prying eyes of his children for 50 years. I offer some of these letters through this book to expand the historical record, to honor my father's service, to honor the service of all the men and women who risked much to defend our freedoms in every conflict and in recognition of those "who also serve who only stay and wait"… or write.

PART I
Learning to be a Soldier

Saturday, September 30, 1944

Dear Mary,

By this time you probably know I'm a private in the U.S. Army. Although I'm very disappointed not being a sailor, I've decided to be a good soldier. So far I have no complaints in any way, shape or form.

I'm writing this letter from the Bell Telephone Center at New Cumberland, PA. I just tried to call my mother but she wasn't home at the time and I spent the time talking to Catherine[1].

This is the first decent chance I've had to write a letter for it is the first free time we had since arriving. I wrote a letter to home while confined in the barracks and if the folks can read the horrible writing they'll know a little about how I look at Army life. It can be summed up in a very few words. I'm here because it's my duty to be here, because I must be here and because I live in the finest country in the world.

The thing that really surprised me most was how authentic were all the stories I read and movies I've seen on the subject of a recruit's first day in the Army. In my letter to the folks I described how disheartened we were and how the typical birdbrains of some cheerful recruits lifted our spirits with wisecracks, jokes and peculiar habits. One of the first incidents reminded me of the movie, "Private Hargrove." Not far out from Philly, a recruit broke out a carton of cigarettes and started peddling them up and down the aisles.

I also told the folks about the butterflies playing havoc inside my stomach. This is largely due to imagination. For when you don't know what's going to happen next you can imagine almost anything. A good example of this is best illustrated in a little story.

---

1 Catherine is Andy's younger sister.

A German officer, a young lady, a Romanian private and an old woman were riding in a train. The train went through a tunnel and everything was dark when was heard the sound of a kiss and then a terrible wallop. When the train emerged from the tunnel the German officer had a black eye.

Thought the old woman – My, what a fine courageous young girl she is to respect her rights as a lady even with a German officer.

Thought the young girl – How strange for him to try to kiss the old woman instead of me.

Thought the German officer – My how smart the Romanian is to kiss the young lady so that I would take the blame.

Thought the Romanian – Oh boy! Am I smart to kiss the back of my hand, sock the German officer and get away with it.

So you see what not knowing has happened, or what is going to happen, can lead to?

The food is swell and they treat us fine but so far the Army isn't as military as I expected it to be. But I guess they're taking it easy on us for the first couple of days. My time is getting short and I want to try and call home again so for now I'll say goodbye and God bless you and your mother and all the folks who had a hand in making my stay at Quaker[2] pleasant.

Your Semi Pvt., Andy

---

2   During the summer of 1944, Andy worked for Quaker City Rubber Company, a job arranged by Mary Jane Waterman, who was executive secretary to the president and vice president of the company.

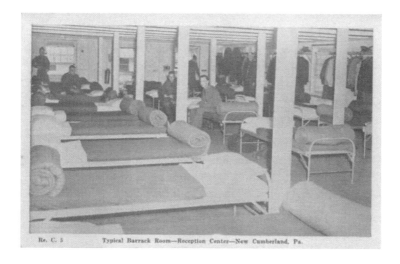

Re. C. 5   Typical Barrack Room—Reception Center—New Cumberland, Pa.

Thursday, October 5, 1944

Dear Mary,

This is Thursday, October fifth, my 7th day here. It is very unusual to be here more than five days but then I'm a very unusual character. If by some unusual circumstance I'm not shipped out tomorrow or Saturday I rate a day and a half of leave and there is only one place I will head. If need be I'll run the whole way to get home. The Army's far above all my expectations but I love Burholme too much to be crazy enough to want to stay away when not necessary.

The last two days we've been kept very busy. Wednesday we had K.P. for fourteen straight hours without a rest. And I used to kick about working nine hours at Quaker. My experience doing K.P. wasn't at the time very pleasant, but now I look back on it as a necessary experience and it will remain with me as a worthy memory.

This seems like a very nice post and I wouldn't mind a permanent assignment right here. On the post we have everything; a movie house just like those in the city, comics and all; a bowling alley; pool parlor; show house; ball field; basketball court (indoors) and a swimming pool. All these things make me wish for an assignment here but above all New Cumberland is only 110 miles from Burholme[3] and the folks and your mother and yourself and Spunky[4].

I can't think of anything else to write. So long for now. I hope you miss me.

Semi Pvt., Andy

Andy and Spunky

---

3   Burholme was Andy's home town in the North East section of Philadelphia.

4   Spunky was Mary Jane's dog.

Friday, September 29, 1944

To - My Andy Bergner

Gosh only knows his correct title – it is now 12:30 – and I don't know how far he has been promoted by this time. Anyhow – this legal document is sent as a contract more-or-less covering one Mary Jane Waterman corresponding to one Andrew Leo Bergner Esquire, DD, MD, DDS and all the other degrees he has secured by his own abilities. So - Andrew is in the United States Army. I'm glad only from the sense that you will be released upon the end of the War – whereas the fleet will have to be manned – the Navy will have to continue on – Japan may be a problem child for the Navy for some time to come. And foremost – it must be fate that led you to that branch of service. Your mother and dad have prayed hard for you Andy, and their prayers for you to be placed where you will be most safe must be answered in this way.

Don't feel that this disappointment is too great. Life is made up Andy of disappointments great and small. We must remember the happy moments – the joys – the real joy of living, otherwise our disappointments will paint a dull grey background in our memory book. Live for today – each day when you get up you will know you are another day closer to home and your friends. Hey – I am getting away from the purpose of this document – it is a contract covering our correspondence – but my belief is that our friendship will cover that.

It is now Monday noon – October 9th.

Your brother Joe came in Saturday afternoon with some baking that your Mother had prepared in hopes that you would be home for the weekend. She made and saved so many things for you and was so disappointed when your Dad called up New Cumberland and found you had left Saturday. When Joe came in Saturday I immediately reminded him that it was the first time he had been in and he said that it was Gump's[5] territory and he wouldn't trespass. So I guess you know your brother is really afraid of you. I joined your family at breakfast yesterday to try and take your place because I know how disappointed they all were. They were not the only ones – my mama had baked a chocolate cake too.

---

5 Andy's nickname was Gump from the Andy Gump comic strip.

I only wish there were something I could do to clip - off Hitler and his whole gang. One hears so many stories and versions of everything that all we can do is hope and wait. There must be a reason – I dunno! Your Aunt Olga was telling me yesterday that the Priest had said in his sermon that it was very difficult for them because so many people are questioning God and stopping their church - going saying that there isn't a God otherwise we would not have a terrible war taking children away from their homes. But he explained that there was a reason behind it all – too great a reason for us to understand – that some of the other people of the world are subjected.

I got a bright idea – when you write to me, if you would care to mail it here at the office I would get it in the morning instead of waiting until I get home at night. If you would kindly do this – mailing it to Miss M.J. Waterman, c/o Quaker Rubber Corporation, Frankford, P.O., Philadelphia 24, Pa. – marking it PERSONAL down in the left-hand corner – I would appreciate it – because I will be anxiously awaiting every word from you – to know that you are alright. McGovern[6] wanted me to tell you how all the boys are anxious to know about you – that he personally wanted to be remembered to you and wish you all the best luck possible. Do you rate!! I do want to wish you all the best of good luck in all you do. Work hard – you won't be sorry. Try to get ahead but don't let anybody take advantage of your willingness – but be sincere and true to yourself.

MJ

---

6   McGovern was vice president of Quaker City Rubber Company where Andy worked the summer of 1944 before he reported for duty.

CAMP JOSEPH T. ROBINSON
Little Rock Arkansas

Wednesday, October 11, 1944

Dear Mary,

I hope by this time you've learned where I am. This isn't such a bad camp but it gets too cold at night and too hot in the day to suit me. Even if this Army can't make a man of me they'll at least give me dishpan hands and housemaid's knees. They are a very particular lot and they demand the barracks spick and span. Our beds must be made so tight that a half dollar will bounce six inches high off them. Our clothes must be hung on hangers with all buttons buttoned. If you wish to send me something, send old clothes hangers. I could use them.

The training we are receiving and are about to receive is very tough but that isn't what bothers me. I could even enjoy this training and I sometimes do whenever I forget about home. But my home and friends I don't wish to forget because I am too damn soft. At any rate I will be home in four months to see if they still remember me. So long for now.

Andy

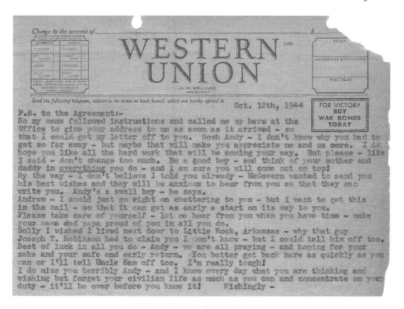

Sunday, October 15, 1944

Dear Mary,

Yesterday Army life brightened up very much. It wasn't because they worked us any easier, in fact yesterday was the toughest day we've had so far. The cause of my boosted morale and inexhaustible energy was mail. I received three letters, one from my mother, one from Kate[7] and your very encouraging letter. Naturally, I read Mom's letter first and Kate's next, saving yours till last because it was much more lengthy than the others. I realized I couldn't have picked a better order in which to read them. Mom's letter did its job by giving me that sense of responsibility necessary. Kate's letter lifted my spirits with that certain something you could only get from one's sister. Then your letter, with its flattery, made me feel self-confident and important.

So, you'd like to take a crack at Hitler would you? Well you can do your share at Quaker and by writing to me and giving me the encouragement necessary to deal with the Hitler gang because I have an idea I'll be in on that messy affair.

Those people you speak of who leave the church and blame God for this terrible war are very narrow minded. Our Lord probably could put a stop to the war instantly, but we were put on earth by our Savior to work out our own existence, "by the sweat of thy brow thou shalt eat." Man got himself into war and it's up to man to pull out. How do I feel about war? Well you know your peace loving Andy who likes Burholme so much. I feel this war was declared by legal authority and that I act at the will of my superior, the Commander-in-Chief and using my own conscience of course, any act done by me must be answered for by that Superior.

Your, Andy Bergner

---

7   Kate was the nickname for Andy's younger sister Catherine.

Camp Joseph T. Robinson in North Little Rock,
Arkansas, is the home of the Arkansas National
Guard. During WWII the post became an infantry
training replacement center. In addition to
training U.S. Troops the camp housed up to 4,000
German prisoners of war. Camp Robinson was
regarded nationally as a model POW camp. Living
conditions were pleasant and included barrack
housing, recreational activities, creative and
educational opportunities. Soccer was popular
and the prisoners performed theatrical plays
and musical concerts. All POWs were required to
work in the camp or on surrounding farms or local
construction projects. POWs were paid .80 cents a
day and could use their wages in the camp store to
buy toiletries, candy, cigarettes and even beer.
The fair treatment experienced by German POWs
had a lasting impact on them. After repatriation,
many former prisoners returned to the United
States to launch professional careers or to renew
acquaintances with their former captors.

Andy has no memory of encountering POWs at camp.

Monday, October 16, 1944

Dear Mary,

   Today I was the most envied and happiest fellow in the whole camp. I received eight letters and a package from you. I certainly wish to whole heartedly thank you for your wonderful correspondence set and money belt. I am writing this letter down in the latrine because lights are out in the barracks. This isn't a very good place to write so I will say God bless you.

Andy

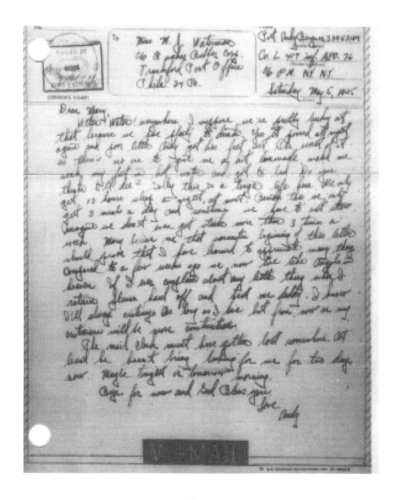

Thursday, October 19, 1944

Dear Mary,

I don't know just what to do with you. Don't you know it's not right to ridicule the government's device for assuring prompt delivery of oversees mail. That little device called V Mail is very important because of its effectiveness, promptness and assured delivery of mail to fellows overseas. It enables important letters to reach our brothers-in-arms before they have a chance to get disgusted.

So what do you do, you poke fun at everything about the idea. Maybe you're one of the folks that don't like the idea because you can't "right" enough. Well if one letter isn't enough, write two or even three. Now that you've received your bawling out, let's get down to the business of the day. Thanks for the hangers. I sure can use them.

It's not hard to make friends in the service. We're all fellows approximately the same age and we're all here for one purpose. Mary, you just don't realize how lucky we are to be living in America until you really take time to think about it. On K. P. yesterday, 17 hours of it, I had plenty of time to think. It's really worth fighting for.

This training is very tough and I am getting fairly tough myself. Now don't get me wrong, I'm still the same old Andy, I am just taking care of myself a little better. Yes, it was tough leaving home but it was a necessity and home is very close to me always. I'm always thinking of nothing but home when I have nothing else on my mind. It's probably some special grace granted to me but when on the drill field, my mind goes blank to everything but things military. With such mental coordination I probably won't go wrong. It's pretty late so I'll say good night. God bless you, your mother and Spunky.

Andy

Saturday, October 21, 1944

Dear Mary Jane,

Today we received three more shots. At New Cumberland
we got two which were supposed to have an after effect but didn't
bother me. The shots we received today are quite a nuisance.
When the doctor stuck me I felt nothing whatsoever, in fact,
I stood there until he asked me if I wanted seconds. Before I
reached the door to get out I thought my arm would drop off.
Well that left arm pain has left but the right arm is now going
through hell. Oops, I'm sorry it's the environment.

So, you are getting disgusted with the great number of
leaves blowing in your yard from the Bergner's trees. If I were
home I could help you clean the place up a bit. Here in Arkansas
I noticed for the first time the real beauty of the turning leaves.
The majority of trees here are oak and persimmon. These two
trees probably have the greatest variety of colors when the leaves
start to turn than any other pair of trees. The more I look around
this camp, the more beautiful it seems. Mary, you tell me to keep
smiling – well I can't help it. Smiles seem to be natural with me.
Can you imagine what makes me so happy when I should be sad
because of the 1,400 miles between my friends and I? Well, I can't
either but it's there.

Your loving friend

Andy

Tuesday, October 24, 1944

Dear Mary,

It's Tuesday night and the moon is shining fairly bright. I can't say it's raining because I wonder if it ever rains in Arkansas. The ground here is so hard it caused the shells from eight inch guns to bounce back. Last night we had a two hour class in the G.I. bill of rights and they tried to explain to us the approximate procedure for discharge. The Lieutenant wasn't very optimistic. He figures most of us will be used in the war against Japan or to police Europe. If I have my choice, I'll take my chances with Japan because this occupation Army idea doesn't interest me at all. To get home as quickly as possible is all I care about right now.

They have ping pong tables in the day room here but as yet I haven't found time to waste in such a manner. About that present I promised to ask for, it's pretty hard to decide on something you need for, if necessary, you can do without almost anything. Oh! This correspondence set has an empty picture frame in the back of it. It is approximately five by seven. That is something I could ask for which would keep me in constant memory of you.

Mary, how do you read my mind? I think many times we both arrive at the same conclusions at the same time. The way you advise me to look on army life is exactly the way I have decided it shall be with me. I'm running short of time and paper so good night and God bless you.

Andy

P.S. Don't forget that picture.

Thursday, October 26, 1944

Dear Mary,

By multiplying your joy by about ten or twenty times you will realize how overjoyed I am when I receive mail from you. It's mail from home that keeps us going with a big grin. You needn't feel sorry for me and my dishpan hands. Just think of the lucky girl someday.

Mary it's all right to do a certain amount of arguing about the outcome of the game on Thanksgiving Day[8], but you are only giving Kate more rope with which to hang you. Mom tells me that my friend Grace sided with you in the argument. She doesn't have very good taste in school football teams even if she did graduate from Frankford. My prediction still goes - 25 to 0.

So long and God bless you. I suppose you get tired of seeing the God bless you on all the letters but I really mean it. Your "best" friend,

Andy

---

8   Annual football rivalry between Andy's Alma Mater Northeast Catholic High School and the nearby public high school, Frankford, from which Mary Jane graduated.

Saturday, October 28, 1944

Dear Mary,

Speaking of needles we got an additional one again today. Again I waited for seconds but the Doc just wouldn't give them to me. My left arm is now pretty stiff but it will be in shape to go to town tomorrow. Yes, the storm has now spent itself and I have passed all the obstacles and can go to town tomorrow to see what Little Rock really looks like instead of looking at post cards. Before getting permission to go to town we had a very rigid inspection of everything such as military courtesy, General Orders, rifles, clothes, equipment, barracks and personal appearance. Last night I didn't write you so I could devote a maximum of time to taking care of all these chores.

This morning we had to go through the confidence (obstacle) course. You have heard of obstacle courses, well this is just what the name states. It is a confidence course – you really need confidence to go over it. Well I figured other fellows before me did and the government would bury me if I broke my neck so I just did everything in the prescribed manner. But it seems some fellows didn't and this lack of confidence was noticed and objected to by the C.O. After we finished running, the night after the course, he informed us there would be no passes this weekend because about half the fellows fell out and failed to finish. This was a surprise to me because I finished third. When the fellows received this news it brought cussing, dissention and gloom down on us. It didn't have much of an effect on me because I don't know anyone in the town anyway.

Anyway, after we had rifle inspection, and those rifles were spotless because of all last night's preparation, the C.O. commended us on that and proceeded to inspect the also spotless barracks. That pleased him also and he made us spend the afternoon studying General Orders. Just a few minutes ago he gave us the good word. No passes tonight but we can go to town tomorrow. I was glad because it proved my point. When the fellows started their cussing, I told them first impressions are probably and usually wrong.

Tomorrow after mass I expect to go to Little Rock. I don't know what I'll do but I'd like to have my picture taken and get weighed if possible. Well so long and God bless you. Give my regards to all.

Your friend, Andy

Monday, October 30, 1944

Dear Mary Jane,

Today, along with a package and eight other letters I received your very unusual letter. It attracted quite a bit of attention in the barracks. The fellows kidded me by saying it was the Declaration of Independence. I don't think they were far wrong. Call it what you will but the back of that sheet should be an historical document because it states the truths in so far as this generation, of which I am a part, is called upon to band together to preserve the independence that many intelligent men of much foresight brought about by their fearless courage many years ago.

Mary you can tell Spunky they have dogs in Arkansas but she's got it all over the best of them. As we march along, maybe two or three dogs who wander the post will follow us up barking as they go. Well Mary Jane it's getting late and I must get some sleep, we have a very long day tomorrow from 6 a.m. to 11:45 p.m. So long and God bless you.

Your loving friend, Andy

Tuesday, October 31, 1944

Dear Mary,

This sure is a busy day. We should have had time off this afternoon but we had 3 periods of mapping and 1 period of exercise on the confidence course. This letter will be interrupted once more. The Sarge just came in for four more volunteers to carry equipment to class tonight. We are to be planting anti-tank mines tonight from 7:15 to 11:30 pm. Well anyway, he asked for four volunteers – you, you, you and you – and I was the you close to the door he entered. I must report in about 8 minutes so be patient. It won't make any difference to you will it? Maybe I should make you pause at the points where I stop writing and wait the four hours before continuing to read the letter?

Here I am again at 11:30 and no worse except that I'm a little more tired than four hours ago. We planted a mine field and then had to dig up a mine field planted by another platoon. I'm in the 1st platoon and naturally we made out the best. In the field we planted, many, many mines went off when the other fellows tried to remove them. In the field we dug up, no mines were set off. That is quite a record and if we could do that in combat, the war would be over very soon.

I received your card and note from Long Island City this morning. Today's letter was No. 9. Thanks a lot. So long Mary, I must write home. God bless you.

Your loving friend, Andy

Friday, November 3, 1944

Dear Mary Jane,

Again today the fellows were very much amused when they spotted me in my secluded corner reading your very swell and unusual letter. Gosh you sure write encouraging and interesting letters. I hope that someday I may be able to draw some interest through my pen. Your pen name should be Mary Jane Greenleaf Waterman.

Yes, Madge[9] got 60 birthday cards but none from her brother Andy. However, I wrote her a letter the day after her birthday. I'm awfully forgetful. Maybe you'd be good enough to remind me of my Mother's 27th wedding anniversary on January the 28th (I think). Madge is very faithful to me. I'm ashamed to say even much, much more faithful than I am to her. Everyone seems faithful to me in my period of trial and regimentation.

There are so many different subjects and types of subjects in this Army life that it will hold my interest for the seventeen weeks[10]. The way they have our schedule worked out helps too. They don't have a daily routine. Every day we have a different subject or two and these subjects don't run in any weekly sequence. Each day we are kept in suspense until the class begins. This also helps add interest and you might say adventure and thrill to this life.

Well Mary, I've bored you far too long. So long and God bless.

Your very best friend, Andy

---

9   Andy's elder sister Magdalene

10   Period of basic training

Saturday, November 4, 1944

Dear Mary Jane,

You know, I think you're a republican the way you talk about my Commander-in-Chief. Now it's only natural for me to try and give you an argument by taking up for Roosevelt. After next Tuesday you'll realize you must put up with him for four more years.

Mary, on Tuesday night here the moon was very, very beautiful and inviting. It was a homesick moon, it made me homesick. Some mornings when I wake up I feel as if I am home and unconsciously reach for the radio switch on my right hand side. I can't understand why because this place is nothing at all like home.

Well Mary, so long for now. Keep arguing with Kate, keep writing to the "Bergner Boys"[11] and God bless you.

Your very true loving friend, Andy

---

11 Mary Jane wrote to several service men throughout the war including Joe and Fritz Bergner, Andy's brothers.

Wednesday, November 8, 1944

Dear Mary,

The Arkansas dust which has proved so much of a nuisance isn't half as bad as the mud. It's all the same soil but what a difference a night's rain can make. This is Mortons Salt country. Did you ever double-time for about a mile in the pouring rain? I did. Ha Ha, that's one on you. Here's the story. Yesterday at 3:30 P.M. the sun was brightly shining, the dark clouds moved over about 3:45 p.m. and at 4:00 p.m. the outburst commenced in all its fury. Within 10 minutes the remarkable transformation took place. This fellow here was a very lucky boy yesterday. I was on K.P. in the shelter and warmth of the Mess Hall while the fellows were on a sixteen mile hike. The rain made their packs twice as heavy on their backs and the massive puddles and beating rain didn't help matters any. They sure were a tired and dejected lot when they finally marched in. However, I still sort of wish I could have had the experience. It might have proven worthwhile later on.

This morning the rain was still coming down. Luckily we had all inside classes today except one. This one was physical instruction. They left us off easy by letting us run around a little bit then showing us a movie. We go on an overnight march starting tomorrow morning and returning Friday night. I'll receive no mail and answer no mail in this period. The goodies you sent will have to wait for me till Saturday. Don't worry and don't let my Mother worry about me over Thursday and Friday because no matter how wet it is I'll enjoy myself. Why do I like the rain?

If Kate suggested to you that N.E.C.H.S.[12] would lose the Thanksgiving Day game due to the loss of 5 players I had better reinform her. It isn't an individual player that wins for my Alma Mater. They work as a team. Maybe the score won't be as high but they'll surely win, for me.

You only hoped Dewey would get to be elected so you must bear with the great white Father for four more years. If you had real faith in your choice, I mean real undoubting faith that he would win, he would now be in line for President.

I haven't much faith in that Zodiac foolishness but it did arouse my interest enough to look up the word procrastinate. When I found out it meant to put off from day to day I had to agree but I don't think it very serious in my case. My work always gets done sooner or later. So long Mary Jane, take good care of Quaker, your mama, Spunky and all the rest of the folks. God bless you all.

Your procrastinate friend, Andy

---

12   North East Catholic High School

Friday, November 10, 1944

Dear Mary,

Last night I received and read your letter under unusual circumstances. We were out in the hills on bivouac somewhere in Camp J.T. Robinson, Arkansas. We had just pitched our tent in total darkness when mail call was sounded. I got four letters and had to build a fire in order to read them. I got a letter from my brother Joe and he confessed all about his experience with his new Italian lady friend from Norwich. We are true brothers and keep no secrets from one another so I can't razz him for his Italian taste. Italians are pretty nice people. About 6 of my newly acquired friends are Bambino's grown up. After reading these letters I felt awful because I couldn't answer them. However, I managed to get a letter written and smuggled out to be mailed home even after dark.

I enjoyed the type and conditions of our training in the last two days so much. It was Utopia lying on my stomach in the tall golden grass with the sun beating on my back while I wrote to the folks on a piece of carefully guarded paper balanced on the butt of my rifle. The classes held yesterday were very interesting. Today I had to march nine miles in order to receive your letter. There was also a letter from Marjorie Levering as well as three from the family.

It sure does please me that Rita is now a very good friend of the entire Bergner family. The only thing wrong is that I was not there to do the introducing. Maybe I could have talked Rita into teaching me to dance or play ping pong. There's no sense in having fellows teach you, that's no fun. Grace taught me to dive and that was fun.

Mary to prove I am all out to have my character remain the same as when I left Burholme, I have started a heckling scheme. Every time the fellows use immoral language I shout out, "Watch your language." At first and at present this meets up with many and varied wisecracks, but now I am not alone. A couple other fellows around here also have a conscience. Since tonight we have a barrack rule. Any fellow who uses carelessly immoral language must buy all the fellows present a coke. It really has done some good. The situation was really getting awful.

I certainly do realize my parents are always near me. I can never make a decision without first being sure of what my Dad would do. Mary, every animal loves my Dad for he loves animals and animals are really good judges of character. I must clean my rifle so I will say God bless you.

Andy

Sunday, November 12, 1944

Dear Mary,

Today I received and was pleased with your newest document. Please discard your wonderful writing paper and continue with your very original ideas. What do I care what the fellows say. They're just jealous anyway. The latest wisecrack is, "Where is the wall that calendar was on?" They are still waiting for the toilet tissue issue.

Mom sure did place a stamp of approval on Rita. The Watermans, Wellivers and Bergners must be good friends by this time. I hope Rita hasn't forgotten me already. Tell Mr. McGovern that I also wish to be remembered to him. He probably can get the work done now without me as a drawback.

I'm still smiling for I enjoyed myself in Little Rock today. Maybe it was the fellow I was with. Mary, I don't like that amber fluid but "When Andy comes marching home" he sure will be very sociable. So long and God bless you.

Your very loving friend, Andy

Monday, November 13, 1944

Dear Mary,

Today I received the copy of "The Sad Sack" you sent. At first I thought you implied that I was a Sad Sack but then I opened to the front page and saw the inscription you inserted, "to the finest soldier in the world." Mary today I'm afraid I proved that a misstatement. Today we went on the rifle range and Andy doesn't take after his older brother Joe. Out of 24 shots I scored 5 bull's - eyes and only 87 points of a possible 120. That is average but some fellows scored 98 to 102.

I didn't miss the target completely but to be an expert rifleman you should score 105 points. Maybe I'll improve with practice but being a lefty, I'm at a disadvantage with the Garand Rifle. Of course the fact that I never fired a rifle before may have something to do with it but that bulls - eye sure looked like about half a dot from where I was firing. It's late so goodnight and God bless you Mary.

Your very best friend and thankful soldier boy, Andy

Saturday, November 18, 1944

Dear Mary,

It's 7:50 p.m. and it's really raining outside. I intend to go to the second show at the regimental theater tonight. The picture is "Princess and the Pirate" with Bob Hope. It will be the first show I have seen on the post since my arrival. Today we had it very soft but tomorrow I can't go to Mass as I am accustomed because I must pull targets for the fellows who aren't such good shots with their M1 rifles. Yes, Mary I made it. Andy tried hard and not only qualified as a marksman but as a sharpshooter. I am not an expert but at least a little better than the average. I just couldn't let Joe show me up in fear he would become your favorite because of my poor soldiery. Well bye now Mary. I think I'll go to that show and get a few laughs before my Sunday work. God bless you and all.

Your loving G.I., Andy

Monday, November 20, 1944

Dear Mary,

I was just writing your Mother a note of thanks in the name of the fellows and myself for the delicious cake I received in this noon's mail. While I was folding the paper one of the fellows barged in with another package. The fellows can't understand how I have so many swell friends but are always glad and anxious when Bergner gets a package. Everyone was very pleased to see and smell the peanuts. Now they are all busy seeing who can eat the mostest the fastest. The only trouble is we will have a mess to clean up when we are through. Time out – I've gotta get in on this – after all you addressed them to me. I'll say thanks for the swell letter and the peanuts. So long and God bless you.

Your loving friend, Andy

November 1944

Dear Soldier Boy,

Not knowing Uncle Sam's ability to deviate from his good reputation – in the delivery of mail – I want to be sure to get THIS letter to you – which I truly wish I could tell you in person.

Yes – Andy – we who live in the United States must pause from our daily tasks to realize the things for which we must be most thankful. We should be thankful to our God that we have freedom to do many things that are denied in many parts of the world. We here may worship as we please – express our thoughts as we please – do as we please so long as it does not interfere with other people and we may advance by virtue of our own ability. Of course, I am not in the Service – I am very much at home – for this Thanks-to-be-given Day, but in thought I am with you.

In 1621, after their first harvest, the first Thanksgiving of the Pilgrim Fathers welled from the hearts of men who were also determined that liberty and freedom should live – just so determined are we this Thanksgiving. We must be thankful for the Country of which we are a part – for our friends – and for the privilege of LIVING.

This old American custom shows up the real heart and soul of an American. Even in the midst of War, with millions of our citizens scattered to the four winds of the world, we still observe this Special Grateful Day which brings to our memory lane the American Poet's words:

"Our Father's God, from out whose hand
The centuries drop like grains of sand.
We meet today, united, free,
And grateful to our land and Thee.
To thank Thee for the era done
And trust Thee for the opening one."

This day set apart gives us an opportunity to pause in reflection at the true significance of this solemn occasion. To every true American it will mean more than a day which marks the observance of religious services and as an occasion for the family reunion, in thought if not in fact. In the troubled world of today we know that each real American will measure up to any privation or sacrifice necessary in the maintenance of our civil rights, our liberty and the privileges we have enjoyed and which we desire to pass on to future generations.

Since the days of the Pioneers it has been customary for families and friends to gather at the family board and partake of all good things to eat and give thanks for God for the bountiful harvest. Tradition has kept alive the custom of gathering and feasting, but perhaps we have lost the most beautiful part of the Thanksgiving celebration; it was the practice of our progenitors, not only to feast, but to gather in front of the fireplace afterward while each in his turn related his blessings for the past year and counted his "thanksgivings." Let's you and me revive the old-fashioned Day of Thanks in all its glory and in its fullest meaning and share our blessings.

I'm most grateful for my wonderful mama – she has patiently guided my steps and watched over the pages of my Book of Life. My blessings are too numerous to share with you – but God's handiwork is displayed in my many friends. Only in the past months have I gathered a family of Bergners in my heart. They represent in my way of thinking the ideal family – true to each other – and bound in the common cause of today's sacrifice. Your mother and dad will have heavy hearts this Thanksgiving Day – they will be thankful of course that you are safe – but just to reach out and touch you would lighten their burden – but Fritz, Joe and Andy are Uncle Sam's temporarily.[13] Mr. and Mrs. America of "7427"[14] deserve the greatest of God's blessings – they have proven their fine characters in their grand family.

---

13   All three Bergner sons were involved in the war effort. The eldest son, Fritz, an employee of the General Electric Corporation, was working for the Army Air Corps repairing and improving aircraft. Joe, two years older than Andy, enlisted in the Marine Corps immediately after Pearl Harbor. After basic training at Paris Island, he was assigned to run a mobile field unit for optical equipment based in Pennsylvania. Later he was sent to officer candidate school at Colgate College where he remained until the war ended. After the armistice he enlisted in the Marine Corps reserves. He was called up during the Korean War but again his duties were stateside.

14   7427 Rising Sun Avenue was Andy's address in Burholme, Pennsylvania

So as we share in thought this November 23rd – we will not consider it a regular Thanksgiving Day – because every day now must be set apart for thanks - giving – so that tomorrow will bring our hearts' desire – the return to normal living.

I am afraid on the evening of November 23rd, 1944 I will have to regret many words spoken during the day. Kate and I are going to the Northeast - Frankford game. Even if either team is noticeably out - played or if they measure even - up, Kate and I will have a feud. Kate fighting for Andy and Joe and poor me, holding my own. You will be with us however, so don't feel as if you are alone in the crowd at Camp Robinson – our sincere prayers will be your very own.

Instead of looking back on what we did last year and the year before – let's plan what we are going to do next year. We must make each day worth the trying – each task or duty successful – we must be honest with ourselves – and the world will come to know us as individuals. We must make our parents proud of their accomplishments only through our accomplishments. Then in our celebration next year we can repay the parental guidance and love – facing the world for them, loving the life instilled in our heart and living the life we love.

I believe I have in some small measure proven my thankfulness for knowing you. Andy – if at any time – in any way – I can do anything possible for you – anything that will add to your contentment and mental relaxation – please call upon me. I shall consider it a special favor to be able to play a small part in YOUR patriotic program. May I always merit the privilege of proving to be your true friend.

Mary Jane

Wednesday, November 21, 1944

Dear Mary,

Boy am I lucky. Yes I'm lying around here again. Why? Well today I received your very swell picture. The boys here are always showing off the pictures of their wives. So Andy here took the liberty of quieting them down by telling them you were my wife when I displayed the picture. It was sure swell and everyone said I was lucky to have such a swell looking woman. Believe it or not I had my picture taken. I was almost laughing when it was snapped and I'll have to wait awhile to see how homely and horrible it is.

Your letter on the occasion of Thanksgiving sure was inspiring. I read it on the bus and on the way to town Monday night. A lieutenant riding the bus smiled when he saw the size of the paper so I invited him to read it. He thought it was swell and couldn't praise it enough. Hope you don't mind.

Well this time tomorrow you will need some cheering up over your Alma Mater's loss. You'll see how really good our team can play, yes even without Willis. Tomorrow is Thanksgiving and we will work eight hours but will have a feast and party from 6:00 o'clock on. Andy was appointed a table waiter because he has no young lady to bring along. That's OK I can drink more G.I. beer. If I succeed in downing a ½ bottle I'll be lucky. You know how I like beer. I'll inform you how I make out. I am also going to try smoking one of the cigars, purely for the amusement of the boys. I may even get sick and not have to hike on Friday. Gold Bricker! Mary Jane, I still must write to Blanche, Rita, Grace and Marjorie and home tonight so bye for now. God bless you.

Your loving G.I., Andy

THANKSGIVING

Thursday, November 23

1 9 4 4

Company "C"

133rd Infantry Training Battalion

Camp Joseph T. Robinson, Arkansas

Company "C"

133rd Infantry Training Battalion

Camp Joseph T. Robinson, Arkansas

ARNOLD J. GORDON
2nd Lt., Infantry Commanding

2nd Lt. Edward A. Assmus	2nd Lt. Walter Robinson
2nd Lt. Carl J. Sklamba	2nd Lt. Allan D. Woodell
2nd Lt. John B. Lippard	1st Lt. Earl J. Rodman

CADRE

1st Sgt. Thomas J. Matthews	Cpl. Paul C. Mendoza
T/Sgt. Lawless L. Burge	Cpl. Truman B. Shults
S/Sgt. Horace R. Booton	T/5 John Berry, Jr.
S/Sgt. Harry M. Kirk	T/5 Hector L. Mallette
Sgt. William H. Carter	T/5 Richard F. Morris
Sgt. Emmitt R. Painter	T/5 Claude Polston
Sgt. Clifford E. Perry	Pfc. Arnold J. Benson
Sgt. Clyde Wallace	Pfc. Joe B. Bratotic
Cpl. Joe V. Cox	Pfc. Henry A. Hickey
Cpl. Louis M. Drozdowicz	Pfc. Arlo D. Paul
Cpl. Harry J. Garrity	Pvt. Creed Ford
Cpl. Joseph F. Hohenwarter	Pvt. Vasco Giuntoli
Cpl. Thomas L. D. Haynie	Pvt. William M. Hill
Cpl. William S. Hawkins	Pvt. Charles M. Tommasi

TRAINEES

Aaron, James E.	Bender, Alfred	Catron, James E.
Abbandando, Lawrence H.	Benedetto, George J.	Ceitin, John E.
Adcock, Andrew B.	Bennett, William L.	Cohen, Jack
Aikins, Harold S.	Bergner, Andrew L.	Cohen, Stanley A.
Anela, Anthony	Bowling, Alfred E.	Cohen, Stanley A.
Antoniak, Julian R.	Braun, Alfred I.	Crone, Vincent V.
Aresco, John	Breuer, Alexander	Cutly, James
Asay, Edward C.	Browning, Vernon H.	Crouse, Ralph E., Jr.
Bailey, William A., Jr.	Bryan, Leon	Currin, Matsh H.
Barnett, James E.	Burke, Harold C.	Cutts, William M.
Barnhill, Otha A.	Burstein, Richard B.	Dacher, Harland
Barry, James J.	Cameron, Harry J.	Davis, Francis M.
Baselice, Joseph N.	Cangelosi, Anthony	DeNapoli, Thomas J.
Bates, Oliver C.	Carey, Miles H.	DeOtto, Edward J.

Friday, November 24, 1944

Dear Mary,

I'm sorry I couldn't write yesterday but was too busy. We worked cleaning up the mess hall until 1:30 A.M. after the party. It is now 8:45 and I just got out of bed. Yes we got a chance to sleep a little longer this morning because of our good deed last night. It was really enjoyable for me and kept my mind away from home and I didn't get homesick. The party was a great success and everyone had plenty to eat including Andy. Did I eat turkey? Man oh man! I even wrapped up a couple drumsticks and have them in my locker now. There wasn't much left but when I saw it being put in the waste can I decided my waste can could use some to.

The reason Andy did table waiting and cleaning last night was so some fellow who wanted to bring his wife could have a good time. He even brought his little 25 month old son. This was the first little fellow I have seen since my regimentation began and I sure do love children. He was so cute he stole my heart away.

Guess what! Andy drank beer and almost liked it. Maybe I was thirsty but it tasted like water to me. We must get ready to go out and meet the Company so I'll say bye for a while. God bless you.

Your loving G.I., Andy

Wednesday, November 29, 1944

Day before Payday

Dear Mary,

Gosh but I'm privileged. Today I received two letters from you. It was my turn at K.P. and those letters certainly pulled me out of the dumps. So you had your nasty old adenoids removed. Honestly, I don't know what they do, where they are located, what they look like or anything so I can't say anything about your operation except that I certainly pray for a speedy recovery and prompt return to Quaker because I don't want to see them shut down.

Don't worry about my taking to the beer. I still like a good chocolate milkshake best. At home beer tasted bad and here it hasn't much of a taste at all. It has been quite a day for me and please forgive such a short letter.

Your loving G.I. friend, Andy

Friday, December 1, 1944

Dear Mary,

Mary I assure you I do not take to "beah" not even 3.2 beah. That was only because it was a very special occasion and I wanted to get in the spirit of things. There are so many celebrations planned for the V-day celebration that everything will cease - transportation and everything. So I think that most of these promises are just wind and will not be fulfilled. Personally it is a foolish gesture. What should happen is a country-wide day of prayer and thanksgiving. Roosevelt on that day should change the date of Thanksgiving to suit the occasion. That's what worries me. Everyone is now full of fear and prayer for a speedy victory but when victory comes they will forget the Almighty Ruler and go about in sin. Is that the way to give thanks? The war news surely has been good lately. Maybe at this rate I won't return a veteran.

Your very loving G.I. friend, Andy

Saturday, December 2, 1944

Dear Mary,

The mailman was very good to me today or rather you folks were. Two packages and eight letters is quite a good deal. There was a package of fruitcake from I'm not sure who. It comes from Local #63 U.R.W.A.[15], 5423 Valley Street, Phila 24 Pa. It sounds like a union and knowing how you love unions you probably had something to do with it. Maybe my uncle, Mr. Lafferty, had something to do with it. I have never belonged to a union in my life. I wish to thank "I don't know who," but I don't know how to go about it.

Tonight and all day tomorrow I have guard duty. You can imagine my attitude when those on guard duty were put on detail this afternoon because the Capt. said, "You can't go to town anyhow." Guard duty didn't depress me because I had figured on this afternoon to write but when I was also deprived of my writing time I was put in a griping mood until I wised up to that fact that this is war. If you care for a weather report from Camp Robinson, this morning I literally froze standing around in the cold. Temperature 18 degrees.

Say, Mrs. Santa Clause, maybe you could steer your reindeers and Santa up to Ryberry Road in Somerton to the Bucher residence. Grace has several brothers and sisters at the age my dad would enjoy making happy. I'll talk to Santa[16].

Your loving G.I. friend, Andy

---

15   Believed to be the United States Railroad Workers Association which has since merged into the Transport Workers Union of America.

16   Every Christmas, Andy's father, Fredrick Bergner, dressed as Santa and delivered presents to the children of family friends. Years later as an adult and father, Andy continued the tradition.

Wednesday, December 6, 1944

Dear Mary,

No rest for the weary this week. I am using up a few spare minutes before chow tonight to write these lines. After chow we start right in again but we only work until nine o'clock tonight. The class last night was a very miserable experience. It should have been interesting and I should have learned something but I let my feelings get the best of me and felt very sorry for myself. It was pouring rain and very cold and we were on scouting patrol wading in the water and mud until eleven o'clock. For those four hours I forgot you folks and very selfishly thought only of myself and worried about keeping warm. Now I realize this doesn't pay and to think of what I have to look forward to after victory is a very good way to forget all these minor difficulties.

This morning we again spent in the rain. Not pouring rain. It has now let up somewhat. Only this morning we were given a break. About 10:30 a jeep came out with hot coffee for us. I never drank coffee but that certainly was good. Using a strong imagination I convinced myself that the hot coffee ran all the way down to my toes and then I was warm all over. This afternoon, thank God, the rain stopped and we fired the Browning automatic rifle. Guess what? I qualified as an expert with it.

I can't understand how my Dad, Russ and you won a game of pinochle over my mother's crew for she is a very good player. Mind if I sign off now, I have about 8 letters waiting.

Your loving G.I., Andy

Saturday, December 9, 1944

Dear Mary,

You may wonder why I didn't write last night. Well I hate to admit it but my wet feet have finally caught up with me. Last night I went to bed after chow with chills and everything else. My judgment proved worthwhile for today I feel fine. The liqueur and pineapple juice from home were also a help.

Down here they give Germany about 16 more days and Japan 10 more months. Very, very optimistic, don't believe it. This last week free time was not to be had in our Company. Our new C.O., Capt. Griffeth is a tough man and doesn't care to give us any breaks. He can give a very natural and convincing smile when he goes with the sad news. Tonight when I finish writing I am going to see the picture "Wilson." So long and God bless you.

Your loving G.I., Andy

Thursday, December 14, 1944

Dear Mary,

The Christmas cards are starting already to pour into me. Today I received six and I haven't even addressed mine yet. Tonight was to be the night but the Army sorta changed my mind. Pray that tomorrow's free time is more free. My cold is now gone. Only a slight cough remains. I suppose at heart I am still the weak young boy of Andy Bergner or "The Bashful Boy of Burholme."

I received two V-Mail Christmas cards from OUR Brother Fritz. I think we are all one family by this time. Now that we have a gate connecting our houses and we are such close friends we are just one happy family. Well good night and God bless you.

Your very loving friend, Andy

Friday, December 15, 1944

Dear Mary,

My plans to write out my Christmas cards tonight went up in smoke because the Capt. had different plans. It's always something around here. Better luck tomorrow I hope.

Today I received your very original letter typed on the paper towel from Quaker. That letter brought back memories. Many times I dried my hands on that kind of towel. Don't worry about me for now, the weather is clear and for two days straight it was actually warm. Funny thing about waddling in the rain and mud, the worst part is thinking about it. After you have had a thawing out and a couple hours rest, you forget all the discomfort and the next little joy makes you all the happier. Thanks for reminding me of Joe's birthday on Monday. Please continue this practice of reminding me in time for such events if possible. Well good night and God bless you.

Your loving G.I., Andy

Camp Jos. T. Robinson

Little Rock, Ark.

Saturday, December 16 1944

Dear Dad,

We had a whole free afternoon in which I concentrated on and mailed out my Christmas Greetings. I have purchased a card suitable for everyone except the girls and yourself. Well, I can send the girls an ordinary card but for you this is impossible, so in my free hours of circumspection I tried my best to express to you my views and feelings of Christmas in the enclosed poem, verse or whatever it is. I hope it doesn't sound too darn silly because I was really sincere when I wrote it. It is my way and now my only way of wishing to "The Best Dad in the World" a Very Merry Christmas and a Happy, Victorious New Year in which I return home, for I hope that is what you want most.

Your loving son, Andy

P.S. Please take care of things this Christmas, Santa – especially Mom because she is facing a manpower shortage and needs extra moral support. Don't forget the little ones.

I won't be home for Christmas
But you can count on me
To wish you well, Gosh my folks are swell
And to think of home and the Christmas tree.

To think of the meaning of Christmas at midnight Mass
The Altar bedecked in flowers and brass.
The priest with his sermon so holy and true
Is the most wonderful thing that enlightens you.

Then to home and presents and wishes of good cheer
From all the folks to whom you are dear.
To think of dear Aunt Olga and her drink of gin
Of how Dad as Santa gladdens the hearts of Tommy and
Dorothy and Lynn.

Of the dining room table stacked with food
Awaiting the hungry but happier brood.
Of poor dear Mom with the job of carving
Amidst the suggestions and desires of her family starving.

Of the pies after dinner and last but not least
The toasts by Dad, the master of the feast.
The stories and laughs of the good old days
Told by all in very funny ways.

This sure is Utopia and will never cease to be
As long as there are thoughts of Christ and a Christmas tree.
These are the things of which I boast
These are the things I look forward to most.

With those things before you, you now have a reason
For my absence from home during this Christmas Season.
It's worth the fight you can bet your life
I'm betting mine in this gigantic strife.

So dear folks I sincerely assure you that on this Christmas Day
I will not be blue. Some folks call it just plain homesickness,
but there must be another name for this swell, most glorious,
delightful, heartwarming, unselfish feeling. I have so many
memories, I could go on for days but I must save some of these for
Christmas day itself.

Sunday, December 17, 1944

Dear Mary,

Last night I went to the show and saw, "Hollywood Canteen." It was a swell picture and I enjoyed it very much. Today was passed off like any other Sunday. Mass and Holy Communion this morning, mail call, chow, letters, town to mail Mom's Christmas card and back to more letters. Your letter and Christmas prayer sort of made me jealous and I tried to write a little verse home as my Dad's Christmas greeting. I could buy cards for all except Dad. There were none that agreed with me enough to send to Dad so I rit a pome. Not very good and it is against all rules of punctuation but it made me feel good. I haven't mailed it but I will tonight. Every day Santa visits camp with his mail bags. By the time Christmas arrives, my barrack's bag will be full of packages marked "Do not open till Christmas." So far I have been very good with my self-control of not disobeying the seals.

It is hot outside today and this pleases me very much. Army life is swell when the weather is nice. The last few days the sun has been brightly shining and the afternoons warm. If only it would remain this way all winter. Good night for now and God bless you. Lots of love,

Andy

Wednesday, December 20, 1944

Dear Mary,

So you are looking after my family now. Just another thing proving how lucky I was when the Watermans moved to 7431. Honest I'll never be able to thank the Watermans for one tenth of their kindness. Mom writes that she is fine, as did you and also Kate, so there is no cause for me to worry. I guess my Mother has things tougher than I do. She worries about every little thing and I haven't time. All she can do is pray, have faith and hope but I am so occupied that I can, and do, enjoy this life most of the time. How I pity these poor young war brides.

The war seems to be going good now that Fritz's bombers[17] are on the job but the war is far from won. When a single foot soldier like myself thinks about the job ahead it goes on into many years but I hope our mechanized divisions and air force help us a little. Well thank you for everything and God bless you.

Your, Andy

---

17   Andy's eldest brother Fritz worked in the aeronautics division of General Electric Corporation on the B 17 and B 29 bombers.

December 20, 1944

Dear Soldier Boy:

Christmas this year is many things to many people. All over the world our service men and women are thinking of home at Christmastide. The words "Peace on earth good will to men" are strange sounding words in the world today – where peace is but a dream – a goal to be achieved when the job at hand is finished once and for all time.

"Glory to God in the highest and on earth peace, good will to men" so sang the angels on that first Christmas night 1,944 years ago – a night destined to be celebrated year after year through the centuries – and will continue to be celebrated until the end of time. Even in that far-off day there was war. Judea was under ruthless Roman rule. Soldiers were quartered everywhere and it was only a couple weeks later that Herod, fearing for his position, ordered the murder of all male children under two years of age, thus hoping to destroy, "Him who was born King of the Jews." However, I am sure that he, whose birthday we celebrate, is still guiding the affairs of men and sometime mankind is going to be willing to be guided by the principals as set forth so long ago in the injunction that we should "Do unto others as we would be done by."

But, who was it who started the gift giving? Maybe you know – but in case you don't, a Bishop of Lycia, Asia Minor is the fellow. Seems as if St. Nicholas – that was the Bishop's name, knew a poor nobleman with 3 daughters. They had plenty of oomph – but little to eat. So this St. Nicholas went to this nobleman's house and threw a purse of gold through the window. Or was it the door? Anyway, he felt so good about it he repeated it again the next night and the following night too. Word got around. And soon everybody was hurling gold purses through windows on St. Nicholas Eve. But soon a depression must have hit them because folks cut it down to one night and gave candy and cakes and little gifts instead. But the spirit remained the same.

The lasting gifts of love, loyalty, faith, enthusiasm, courage – the sparks from those gifts kindle a fire when lighted and mingled with lots of others whose glow is felt through our loving hearts never to be dulled by time or circumstance. This, Andrew, will mark another first time in your life. Be happy in your heart that God is instilling within your heart the realization and proof of your family's love for you. Life's greatest gifts have been handed to you by your dear parents. It is only through their guidance and loving faith that you are a man in God's care – doing your part and shouldering your gun for Burholme and all the other homes. Be strong and be happy. We will be with you on Monday – but not in person. You're never without us in case you don't know it.

MJ

Thursday, December 21, 1944

Dear Mary,

Another letter from you today - No. 42. Today we received our Christmas present from the C.O. Yes, we had the whole afternoon and evening off to do Christmas shopping but it's a little late now. Anyway the rest was swell and worth millions to me if I had it.

I believe Dr. Pancoart must have a bargain price on tonsil operations the way he goes about hacking people up. You must be getting your cut because you are the one who is leading the way. You mentioned that Santa Claus started visiting you. He has also visited me but you haven't given me much dope about the situation for December 25th. Are you still going to be Mrs. Santa Claus? Is my Dad going to make the children happy as Santa? Please give me all the dope about the outcome, your thoughts and feelings at the sight of the face of the very little ones. Even the very little incidents that give you a thrill.

This is weighing-in time. My present weight is 175 lbs. fully dressed. I am the same as I was when I left home. Thanks again for everything. Bye bye Mrs. Santa.

Your, Dr. Bergner

Sunday, December 24, 1944

Christmas Eve

Dear Mary,

Today as you say was a first for me. What a first. Today, Christmas Eve, I received a very huge package from home with a complete Christmas dinner. The spirit of Christmas I received when I spotted all the Christmas packages in Christmas wrapping almost carried me away to some distant place from where I would have never returned to my reasoning self. But, your letter No. 43, the one of December 20th that told me the real cause, reason and meaning of Christmas, saved me from the catastrophe of taking things for granted. Your letter made me realize the meaning behind those packages.

Yes there is hate in the world and the good are involved with the bad but for the good, war is only a trial. I left home good and I'll return home good. Maybe my table manners will be degraded but I'll still be good inside. Well goodnight for now and God bless you. Thanks again.

Your, Andy

Christmas Day "44"

Dear Mary,

I just couldn't let Christmas Day pass without writing you a few lines. Today was a day of many moods for me. It started pleasant, then my happiness was dampened with homesickness by the words of our regimental C.O. In hopes of coming out of the dumps I saw a show which only made things worse. After the show I had a serious mental struggle for about an hour. I made the mistake of trying to figure out why I had to be away from home.

Well finally I wised up, wrote many letters which made me look at the sunny side once again. In particular the one I wrote to my Pastor made me feel swell because it made me realize my real object in life. It is to get to heaven and with this one thought in mind anything is bearable. Good night for now and God bless you.

Love Andy

Wednesday, December 27, 1944

Dear Mary,

Today I received letter No. 44. Yes, thanks for sending the peanuts that I received yesterday. Thanks also for the Reader's Digest. The first issue arrived today and I already read one of the articles. Mary, I'll owe you a great deal when I return home for good. You will be responsible for my improved intelligence. I hope you had a very enjoyable Christmas as Mrs. Santa. I am awaiting the complete dope.

Please excuse the brevity of this letter. Last night I got to bed about 3 A.M. That's this morning but anyway I'm pretty tired. You said you had ice and snow. Well last night we were out until 2 A.M. and when we came in our helmets were coated with ice and had icicles hanging on them. Our gloves, raincoats and rifles were likewise coated. Don't worry though, I'm getting used to being miserable because last night the rain and cold didn't bother me so much. God bless you and Happy New Year.

Love, Andy

Fredrick Bergner as Santa Claus

December 26, 1944

Dear Andrew,

What a glorious time I had yesterday helping Santa. He said he had written you – but maybe I can add some few details which your family didn't tell you.

Mother and I had dinner at your house on Sunday – I acted up mainly for your ma's sake. Your dear Joe became playful and mussed my hair and it became a real battle – I untied his shoe laces and then succeeded in removing his shoes and socks. Your mother served two small pieces of pie meant for Joe – but he decided that he and I should share it. I sat between your Dad and Joe. We shared it all right – he ate my side and I ate his. I dunno who got most but then your Ma served him another piece and when I tried to get some he held it out in mid-air. While I was busy holding his other hand so he couldn't eat your Dad stole my glass of milk and helped himself to a drink. So between the Bergners I had quite a time. Of course the act was put on for your mother's sake. After fixing the candy for delivery on Christmas we went home to trim our little tree about 9:00 o'clock. About 11 your entire family came over to our house – I set Madge's hair and they left for midnight mass.

Yesterday, I was up bright and early but Santa and his dear wife were still in bed when I went over at 9:15. The plan was we were to leave at 9 but it was closer to 10. To Grace's – our first stop. The kiddies were very happy Santa said but I didn't get in there. Of course where we knew there would be small children I couldn't go in.[18] Madge travelled with us then we went home at noon to gather gifts and Kate and Joe went along.

Really we had quite a time. One little boy wanted to know if Santa got the cup of tea and sandwich – oh yes, of course he did. One little boy insisted he should have a cocker spaniel because he would bring back the ball and lay it down. Your dad tried to tell him that instead of a cocker spaniel he should have a fox terrier. Upon leaving, out front of the house a dirty fox terrier chased your dad so he didn't succeed in convincing the boy.

---

18   This was to keep up the illusion that Santa came down the chimney rather than being driven around in a sedan.

One little girl when asked her name – she said, "I already told you" (no doubt a department store deal). In one home the children had not been down to the basement to their toys and Santa took them down. The trains had not worked last year when Christmas was over so the little boy knew they would work if Santa started them. I do believe Santa said a prayer that they would work – but they did. That little boy wanted to kiss Santa and he said, "Oh boy Santa but your whiskers are warm". We only hoped he wouldn't cling to them.

Santa stopped down to the Quaker cafeteria to see the little girl who has had rheumatic fever. She has been bedfast since September. Was she thrilled – I was down there just a few minutes ago to see her and she told me all about Santa. Her little cousin, a little boy, was there when Santa arrived and said to him, "Santa why doesn't your belly shake like a bowl full of jelly?" Santa said it does and he proved it. So little Helen told me about it over and over again. I do believe Dr. Bergner, Sr. has accomplished a lot.

We stopped all along the way to children who happened to be out. However it was raining and that stopped many gatherings. But when your dad was in one home other neighbors called and all the kiddies were so thrilled. We went to the Seelaus'. Frank, in the Navy, and their son from the Army were there. Also two younger boys. The older son and wife and little boy 18 months came in but he was shy of Santa. Last night we went over to Blanche's[19] and Fritzie received the same gift as Spunky – puppy biscuits. He opened the package himself.

Then we took Joe to the station. He was lucky to get a seat on the train to New York – he took the 9:00 train.

We went down to the Convent at 4th and Vine to see the sister who taught you all in school, St. Dunstan is that her name? They (the sisters) were all very sweet and got a big kick out of our visit. Of course I showed off your picture which is in my wallet. Everywhere we went everyone was very much interested in you.

---

19   Blanche was Andy's sister - in - law, married to his elder brother Fritz. Fritzie was their dog.

Oh Andy, I could go writing forever telling you all of the experiences we had. The kiddies were so thrilled and speechless. I couldn't believe the thrill there is in proving the point of Santa. If only things didn't ever become plain – the little mysteries of youth to remain forever – the spirit of Santa to govern every day for everyone. If only – yes – if only a lot of things. If only you had been home all would be well. Your Mama tried hard to cover her feelings but everyone was so mindful of our innermost wish – if only Andy were here. Well – what's the use of making you realize how important you are.

But I can assure you that Santa Claus was terribly tired last night. He didn't even go to the train with Joe. Madge, Kate, Mama and I went. We picked up a soldier boy on the way and gave him a lift. I wise - cracked with him and Joe and kept your family laughing. Inwardly my thoughts were elsewhere. Then your entire family, dad and all came to my house. It was grand. Again, Andy was missing though he was on the desk.

Joe said last night he wouldn't be home again until the end of February so maybe you boys will be together. Gosh I wish tomorrow was February. I can't thank you enough for my Christmas gifts – but if I can in any measure prove my desire to make you as happy as you can be that is all I ask. I do want you to be content that it is God's plan that you make sacrifices – but next Christmas – and before that – we'll all be together. Happy too!

MJ

Friday, December 29, 1944

Dear Mary,

Today I received your very excellent account of your first adventure as Mrs. Santa. I'll bet you consider it one of your most pleasant experiences. The first year I went out with Santa I had so much fun that I figured by the next time the novelty would have worn off and with it the pleasure. Boy was I wrong. The second year was twice as good as the first and now I am convinced that each year the pleasure will be doubled.

So what is this you tell me about my brother Joe and yourself? You must be a couple of chowhounds stealing each other's food. You shock me. What? Was the celebration a Christmas dinner or a burlesque show? Joe certainly can be the life of the party and help keep things moving if he wants to. I'll bet you all had plenty of that golden Sauterne wine at dinner to carry on the way you did. Gosh, I'm glad you had such a good time. I wish I could keep everybody in stitches the way Joe does when he is in the mood.

How did you like Sister St. Dunstan? She taught me for three years and is very responsible for setting me straight and instilling in me my love of God and my family. She can be a little devil and have her fun too. Did you ever see a more happy, giddy bunch of females?

Mary you should be here to help me with my Christmas sweet assortments from my dear friends and relatives. Tuesday I received six belated packages in the mail from Aunts and Uncles from all over. Now I have food in almost everybody's locker. Folks weren't satisfied at sending a cake or a box of candy. They all sent everything. As a result I have six fruitcakes, six boxes of candy and figs, nuts, and sweets of all kinds.

The way things stand now I should be home around the 10th or 12th of February so see that Joe sneaks home earlier. Well I must write home yet so good night and may God shower you with all his choicest blessings. You deserve them all.

Love, Andy

December 31, 1944

Dear Mary,

Last night I went to town. All that I accomplished in town was a swell steak dinner. That was enough, the trip was worth it. Flash! Andy expects to be home ahead of schedule. One month to go. We are to go on our bivouac next Sunday two weeks ahead of schedule. So please no more packages because it will be impossible for me to receive them while on bivouac. Well good night and God bless you and a Very Happy New Year to you.

Love, Andy

Tuesday, January 2, 1945

Dear Mary,

Yesterday, besides being the Feast of the Circumcision was also pay day for us doughboys. I went to Mass last night, and when I returned the boys were very foolishly getting rid of their pay in a crap game in our barracks, my home, my office and living quarters. They made quite a racket and made writing or even sleeping very tough. Yes today there are many sorry boys in camp. Many boys now lack the necessary funds to go home on a furlough at the end of the month. Need I mention that I still have all my pay to purchase a train ticket the very minute we get the word.

Saturday evening at 5 P.M. we start our two week bivouac. The weather promises to be very ideal. It is now about 0 degrees here, anyway it feels like it and tonight the ground is blanketed with snow. This bivouac will cut down and maybe cease temporarily my correspondence so please don't lose faith in me. When we return from bivouac our training will be over and we should be shipped out a week later. Then home for 10 days (I hope). Time certainly does fly doesn't it? Tomorrow we arise at 3:30 A.M. so I'll hit the sack as soon as possible. So long for a while and God bless you. Hoping to see you soon.

Your, Andy

Thursday, January 4, 1945

Dear Mary,

The last couple days have been spent in figuring out the best ways of making myself comfortable while out on bivouac. Tonight I purchased from Little Rock, a woolen hood to keep my little, I mean big, ears warm, a few pairs of heavy socks and some heatabs. Those heatabs[20] are new to me but if half of the advertisement is true they'll be worth plenty to me when I'm cold and have wet socks to dry and water to heat.

As yet I haven't figured out the problem of writing on bivouac. I'll do my best. At any rate I'll have a pencil and some post cards. So long and God bless you.

Your, Andy

---

20   Heatabs are a dry fuel in tablet form used by campers. The product is still manufactured by the Hatch Corporation.

Monday, January 8, 1945

Dear Mary,

This letter must be short and sweet. It's just to let you know that I am well. We are now on bivouac on Deadman's Hill, 15 miles from our barracks and 1,000 yards across from Clifton Mountain, the highest point in Camp Robinson. It seems that from the top one can see all Arkansas. It certainly is beautiful in spite of the mud.

Andy

Saturday, January 13, 1945

Dear Mary,

I now owe you so many letters that I'll never catch up but I hope you understand my position. I received six letters from you in the past week. Three came today. Our first two days out weren't very pleasant because of the weather but since then it has been ideal. Spring must already have come to Arkansas. Today the sun was shining so bright and so hot that I got a mild case of spring fever. Yes, I got lazy and didn't feel like working. Outside of this case of spring fever I feel swell and why shouldn't I? My love of woods and nature, the fine weather and the good chow makes this a very pleasant experience and from the very scant news we hear from the lieutenant informs us that the war is going very well.

In one of your letters you asked whether you should buy something for me to give my folks for their 27th wedding anniversary. Yes please do. I had hopes to be home by then but if things run according to plan I'll be a few days late.

Do you remember that Quaker pen knife you gave me before I left? Well it has been my most valuable and useful piece of property for the last 4 months but yesterday I lost it. Can you replace it? Just for one day, today, I miss it terribly. It was used for everything from opening letters to cleaning my rifle. If you are interested in knowing how and where it was lost I'll tell you.

Yesterday we had a problem on attack by rifle company with artillery support. I lost my mess kit, knife, my meat can and the pen knife while making the 600 yard series of short rushes to the objective. We must jump up, dash about 15 or 20 yards and then hit the ground, roll over and up again. While doing this you will lose anything not riveted to your body. Well it is getting darker so I must close.

Your, Andy

Sunday, January 21, 1945

Dear Mary,

Just a few minutes ago I heard your voice for the first time in four months. Gosh it was a swell feeling to talk to the family. Maybe before two more weeks pass I'll see all you folks. Yesterday morning at 4 A.M. we returned from our two week ordeal among the elements. Did you ever hike 25 miles? It's not so bad now that it is history. Yesterday I received the pen knife you sent. What service. I only asked for it in a letter written on last Monday. I had no idea that a letter would reach you so soon. Chow Call!

Guess what? We had turkey, plenty of turkey. After eating salmon cakes and dehydrated sausage for two weeks that turkey dinner was swelligent. Right now this place is a rumor clinic. The questions asked are, where are we going and when are we going. Nothing official or definite has been reported as yet. All we know is that tomorrow we start an unexpected week of training. We cannot send any laundry out and no one seems to know anything. We can be shipped out at any time. As soon as I learn anything you'll be informed. Well I have about sixty letters unanswered. I must try to answer a few today. So long for now and God bless you.

Your soldier boy, Andy

Wednesday, January 24, 1945

Dear Mary,

Another day, another letter from you and another day closer
to home. That chocolate cake you wrote about makes my mouth
water already. I suppose Army cooks will never be given the
opportunity to bake any good cake. Tonight I took in a show,
"Can't Help Singing," with Deanna Durbin. It was a very, very
good picture. Perhaps I enjoyed it so much because it was chuck
full of good [word unclear] singing, something very seldom heard.
The Technicolor also added to my enjoyment.

Love, Andy

Friday, January 26, 1945

Dear Mary,

Today was a lucky day for my stomach. In the mail I received two cakes and in Little Rock I was treated to a super duper dinner. My Mother's cake is already gone. Your Mother's cake is about 1/3 gone. Mom's cake was received at noon and devoured at noon, whereas your Mother's cake was received this evening and Andy decided that the fellows who ate his cake at noon weren't very grateful. They loved the cake but once it was gone went to their corners and hoarded their packages.

Of course I don't need anything from these fellows but to me that wasn't considered proper so I have a whole delicious chocolate cake all to myself and a very few choice friends. Please try and understand and forgive my selfishness. The rumor still has it that Monday is the day we head for home. Look out, it's only a matter of days now. So long and God bless you.

Love, Andy

Sunday, January 28, 1945

Dear Mary,

Phoned home today and extended my best wishes and God's choicest blessings. Mom and Dad certainly were pleased with the present you purchased for them in my name. Now I must hurry home to get my debts cleared up. Besides owing you for the presents, I owe Mom money for a few phone calls I reversed charges on. I confess my conscience is guilty and I must pay up.

Tonight a few of us are going to the show. We had a little crap game. Yes, I'm a gambler now too. If you folks can play keno, I figure its okay for me to play checkers and shoot crap. We played only for the change we had in our pockets. Five fellows were in the game and I cleaned them all out. Now that I am the financier, I must treat us all to the movie tonight.

All our equipment is now turned in. There isn't much for us to do so we should have plenty of time tomorrow. Well thank you for taking care of things for me. Good night and God bless you.

Love, Andy

Last day at Ft. Robinson - Andy is second from left

Andy on furlough in February 1945 posing with the women in his life. From left to right front: Mary Jane, Andy, Andy's mother Ida, Andy's aunt Olga Lafferty. Rear: sisters Madge and Kate.

Andy and his father Fredrick Bergner

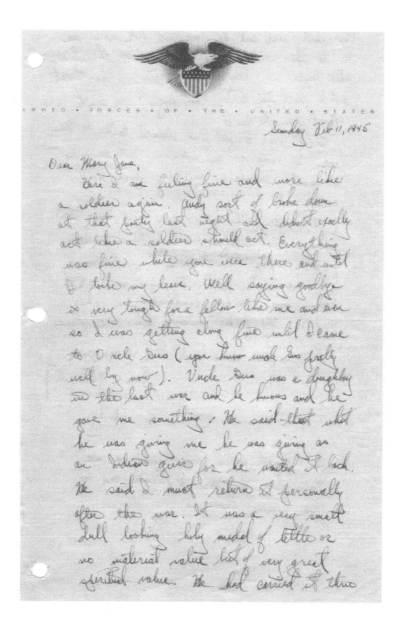

Sunday Feb 11, 1945

Dear Mary Jane,

Here I am feeling fine and more like a soldier again. Andy sort of broke down at that party last night and didn't exactly act like a soldier should act. Everything was fine while you were there and until I take my leave. Well saying goodbye is very tough for a fellow like me and even so I was getting along fine until I came to Uncle Gus (you know Uncle Gus pretty well by now). Uncle Gus was a doughboy in the last war and he knows and he gave me something. He said that what he was giving me he was giving as an Indian gives for he wanted it back. He said I must return it personally after the war. It was a very small dull looking holy medal of little or no material value but of very great spiritual value. He had carried it thru

the last one and he came out OK so I am
to do the same. That Mary is the straw
that broke my big front. Maybe I was tried
but I don't even believe that myself and can't
expect you to can I.

So led home tonight but didn't talk to Mary
Jane. If things go as expected Andy is going
to grash Blanche's birthday party next
week end.

From the folks letter you will learn that
Andy is now enjoying most of the conveniences
of home except the pleasure of your presence.

Tomorrow I will write more as I still
have some turkey sandwiches and cakes
to eat. My folks certainly take care of me.

Bye fore now and God Bless you
Love (lots of it)
Andy

P.S. Eight letters were waiting on me.
Four from a Miss Walerath and one
from Ben Shawcross.
a.

Monday, February 12, 1945

Dear Mary Jane,

Just finished talking to you and I do feel good. I hope that you can come down to pick me up on Saturday[21]. So far it looks as if we will be here long enough for that weekend pass but this is the Army and anything can happen. Saturday night's exhibition was exactly what you said. It really is tough to leave swell folks like you when there is uncertainty about some things in your mind. So far the danger of losing my skin doesn't worry me, but just wait till the shells start whizzing. Mom worries me more than anything but lately she has been a better soldier than I have.

This letter is being written with the Quaker pencil you gave me. Why? Well when I returned to the barracks after making the phone call there was a poker game being played on my bunk and someone was sitting on my footlocker. I didn't want to disturb the game but walked to the P.X., had some refreshments and came here to the day room to write you a letter. You see, I have willpower and am keeping my promise not to gamble; besides I don't know how to play poker. This day room is nice. It contains a radio, piano, ping pong table, dart board, a war news bulletin board with many maps and many books, magazines, paper and writing facilities.

Mary will you be my Valentine, or something like that? Gosh you're swell. Can't concentrate tonight because of the radio. The program is "Thanks to the Yanks." Bye for now and God bless you.

Love, Andy

Fort George G. Meade, still an active Army base in Ft. Meade, Maryland, was a training center during World War II. Its facilities were used by approximately 3,500,000 soldiers between 1942 and 1946. In 1942, the Third Service Command opened the Special Services Unit Training Center, where Soldiers, including swing band leader Glen Miller were trained in all phases of the entertainment field.

---

21 Prior to deployment Andy was temporarily stationed at Fort George G. Meade in Maryland.

Friday, February 16, 1945

Dear Mary,

Well I found myself in a new location again. Things happen fast in this Man's Army so don't be surprised. I know you are wondering where I am and I wish you knew but this is war and Andy's going to live through it so my folks must not know just where I am. We have snow here if that helps any. Saw a lot of familiar territory, even Quaker, among many other things that made me eat my heart out. So near and yet so far. According to the news of the pace the Navy has set for the Japanese war, Andy will get another very, very long furlough soon. Better not write too much for safety sake. Will write more at my next opportunity. So long and God bless you.

Love, Andy

```
Camp Shanks, named after Major General David
Carey Shanks (1861-1940) was a United States
Army installation in Orangetown, New York.
Dubbed "Last Stop USA", the camp served as
a point of embarkation for troops departing
overseas during World War II. It was the largest
World War II Army embarkation camp, processing
1.3 million service personnel including 75% of
those participating in the D - day invasion.
```

Wednesday, February 21, 1945

Dear Mary,

    Well you have no idea how swell it felt when I saw you and especially last night when I sat and talked with you and the folks. I only wish – well you know what I wish. Sorry that little visit was so short but I'm a busy man in certain circles. Soon I'll be a master at saying goodbye instead of the coward I was at the furlough's end. Please keep me posted on how Joe makes out on his leave.

    Gosh how do I rate a friend like you? Just now the war has me on the spot. I accept all of your kindness and cannot repay you, not even a little bit. But when I come home permanently I hope to show you that I am grateful. I won't always be a helpless private depending on my friend's kindness. Please keep writing to me and although I can't promise answers, I can promise my best when an answer is possible. So long and God bless you.

Love, Andrew

P.S. Will write more later.
P.P.S. Don't forget the candy.

Thursday, February 22, 1945

Dear Mary,

Yesterday I was in the dumps but today, after reading once again the poem "Hope" and the letter you sent with it, I again am looking at the bright side of things. Your letters do me so much good in so many ways that should you stop writing it would be a tragedy so please continue and this fellow will never go wrong. Mary, I need your encouragement now more than ever. I would like to say a lot of things but security purposes forbid me from expressing my feelings the best way I know how. This letter was just to let you know that I am still thinking of you and I am still safe and sound. Just wanted to send,

Love from Andrew

P.S. bye for a while, God bless you and pray for me.

PART II
Prelude to Andy's War

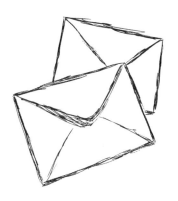

When Andy Bergner was inducted into the United States Army on September 29, 1944, the outcome of the war in Europe was very much in doubt. Allied forces landed on the beaches of Normandy, France, on June 6, 1944, establishing a beachhead on Hitler's fortress Europe at a terrible cost. Allied casualty figures numbered in the range of 10,000. Approximately 2,500 of these were killed in action. U.S. casualties included 1,465 dead, 3,184 wounded, 1,928 missing and 26 captured.

The months ahead were filled with victories, defeats and a seemingly endless stream of casualties. Allied forces finally broke out from the Normandy beachhead and liberated Paris on August 25, 1944. Less than a month later Allied troops advanced to the vaunted Siegfried Line, a defensive system of heavily fortified bunkers, pill boxes, tunnels and tank traps stretching from the Netherlands to Switzerland, designed to protect the western border of the Third Reich from invasion. It represented one of the most significant obstacles to the Allied plans for the final invasion of Germany.

On September 17, 1944, the Allies launched Operation Market Garden, the largest airborne operation of the war. Market Garden was designed by British field marshall Bernard Montgomery to circumvent the northern edge of the Siegfried Line and open the door to an invasion across the Rhine into Germany. It ended in disaster with the Allies suffering more than 15,000 casualties, including the virtual destruction of the British 1st Airborne Division, which lost more than 8,000 men. This defeat shattered any hope that the war would be over by Christmas.

Following the defeat of Market Gardens, the Allies began a series of offensives that proved ineffective against the Wehrmacht. The situation changed dramatically on December 16, 1944, when Germany launched a surprise counter-offensive in the mountainous Ardennes region of Belgium. The resulting Battle of the Bulge represented a desperate last roll of the dice for Hitler and the Third Reich. Initial German victories and a rapid advance westward resulted in heavy losses for the Allies. The climax of the Bulge came on December 26 when General George Patton's Third Army broke through the German lines at Bastogne to rescue the besieged 101st Airborne. In the end, the Germans were unable to sustain their early victories in the Ardennes campaign and they began a long retreat back toward the German border. By the end of January, Allied troops reclaimed every inch of ground they lost during the Bulge.

While American and British forces ultimately prevailed against the forces of the Third Reich, their losses were severe. Allied casualties during the Bulge totaled 76,890 men. German casualties were somewhat less, but the Germans sustained significant losses in equipment and material including the destruction of 600 tanks. Because the Germans could not replace their losses of men and equipment as quickly as the Allies could introduce reinforcements, the Battle of the Bulge would ultimately become the turning point of the war in Europe.

Nevertheless, the forces of the Third Reich remained a formidable and deadly opponent after the Bulge. The Germans had fifty-nine divisions made up of some 462,000 soldiers on the western front in February 1945, facing more than 3.5 million Allied troops on the ground in Europe. Still, the Germans continued to inflict heavy casualties. The average German soldier killed more of the enemy than did the average Allied soldier, but in the end, it did not matter. By the spring of 1945, the Reich had run out of men to fuel the Thousand Year Reich.

In response to the growing shortage of soldiers, Martin Bormann and Heinrich Himmler drafted a proposal for a new national militia or "People's Storm" – the Deutscher Volkssturm. Authorized by Adolf Hitler on September 26, 1944, the Volkssturm was to be comprised of all men between the ages of 16 and 60. Poorly trained and equipped, Volkssturm units had almost no military effectiveness. More often than not, the Volkssturm was used to commit atrocities against fellow Germans who had turned against the Reich or as guards on countless brutal death marches of prisoners being moved from concentration camps lest they fall into enemy hands.

In addition to the terrible losses in manpower, the German forces on the western front were also facing a critical shortage of weapons and materiel. The Allied bombing campaign successfully targeted much of Germany's industrial sector, crippling the manufacturers of tanks, artillery and especially aircraft. As U.S.

troops approached the Rhine in March 1945, the Allies achieved near total air dominance over the western front. Whatever was available in the way of German weapons and ammunition was directed to the eastern front where the Russian army rapidly advanced toward the Oder River and prepared for a final assault on Berlin.

Thus, the Allied forces enjoyed an almost insurmountable advantage on the battlefield. They had 10 times the number of tanks and three times the number of aircraft. Allied artillery outnumbered German artillery by a ratio of 2.5 to 1, and the Allies had a virtually inexhaustible supply of replacement troops. Plus, the weapons carried by the Allies were significantly better. Most GIs carried the M-1 Garand, a semiautomatic rifle chambered for the powerful .30 - 06 Springfield rifle cartridge. Patton called it "the greatest battle implement ever devised." Most German troops, on the other hand, carried bolt-action Mauser KAR 98K rifles, which required the soldier to clear the action by opening the bolt after each shot and then closing the bolt to reload the weapon. In most cases, a firefight between German and American troops was won by the G.I.s.

Still the Battle for the Rhineland proved costly for the British, American and French troops. Terrain and weather frequently worked to the Nazis' advantage. The refortified Siegfried Line, or West Wall as it was also known, represented a formidable obstacle for the Allies. It stretched 400 miles from the Dutch border in the north to the border with Switzerland in the south. The defensive fortification included more than 3,000 "pillboxes" and bunkers armed with machine guns and each containing as many as 70 troops. The entire area, which was between five and 23 miles contained numerous minefields and trenches. One of the most effective elements of the Siegfried Line was the use of rows of "dragon's teeth," massive concrete pyramids between two and five feet tall designed to stop enemy tanks.

The last great obstacle facing the Allied forces after the collapse of the Bulge was the Rhine River itself. A bulwark of German history and tradition since the days of Charlemagne, the Rhine represented the last line of defense for the Wermacht. It was heavily defended, and the situation became even more difficult after the Germans blew a series of dikes and damns

flooding much of the lower Rhine valley between Holland and
Germany. The Rhineland campaign would become the last killing
ground in the West, resulting in enormous casualties on both
sides. The Allied strategy devised by Supreme Allied Commander
in Europe, General Dwight D. Eisenhower, was to attack the
Rhine along a broad front. British, Canadian and American
forces led by British Field Marshall Bernard Montgomery would
attack in the north from the area around Nijmegen, Holland,
cross the Rhine and then strike at the vital Ruhr industrial region.
In the center of the line, General Omar Bradley's massive U.S.
12th Army Group, comprised of the U.S. First Army under the
command of Lieutenant General Courtney Hodges and the U.S.
Third Army under the command of Lieutenant General George
Armstrong Patton would advance to the Rhine through a heavily
wooded region known as the Eifel. At the southern end of the
line, Lieutenant General Jacob Devers commanding the U.S. 6th
Army Group would attack German defenses around the town of
Colmar near Strasbourg, the so-called Colmar pocket. Then his
U.S. Seventh Army would attack the heavily industrialized Saar
region and the Palatinate before advancing to the Rhine.

The attacks commenced on February 8, 1945, as
Montgomery's forces launched Operation Veritable along the
German - Dutch border. To the South Patton's Third Army
assaulted German defenses between the Saar and Moselle rivers
near the town of Trier in Luxembourg. Farther south, Dever's
Sixth Army group cleared the Germans from the Colmar Pocket
and gained control of the west bank of the Southern Rhine River.
The turning point of the campaign occurred on March 7 when
American troops of the Ninth Armored Division of the U.S. First
Army captured the only bridge across the Rhine not destroyed by
the Germans. The Ludendorff Bridge at Remagen would become
the first of several crossing points established by Allied forces.
More than 8,000 American soldiers crossed the bridge during the
next 24 hours, signaling the beginning of the Allied advance into
Germany.

Patton's Third Army first crossed the Rhine near Oppenheim
on March 22. He boasted that the Third Army could now cross
the Rhine at will. To prove his point he staged several additional
crossings at Boppard and St. Goar. Over the next several days
the rest of Patton's Army including the 76th Infantry and Andy

Bergner crossed the Rhine at different points. Two days after Patton's initial crossing, Montgomery's forces finally crossed the Rhine at Wesel. Patton was so elated that he beat his British rival across the river that he stopped midway across the bridge, got out of his jeep and took a leak in the Rhine. In his report to General Bradley, Patton declared, "Without the benefit of aerial bombardment, ground smoke, artillery preparations or airborne assistance, U.S. Third Army at 2200 hrs, Thursday evening 22nd March, crossed the Rhine."

Recognizing the obvious, Hitler finally gave his approval for the withdrawal of all German troops across the line on March 23. By then it was too late. Most of the German troops had already retreated across the river, were captured, or were killed by advancing Allied forces. The cost was been enormous for both sides. German casualties totaled approximately 90,000, including some 52,000 taken prisoner. Allied casualties were far less although still significant. Nearly 23,000 Allied soldiers were killed, wounded or missing in action. The sacrifices of these valiant men and countless others made possible the invasion of Germany and the ultimate defeat of the Third Reich.

PART III
War in Europe

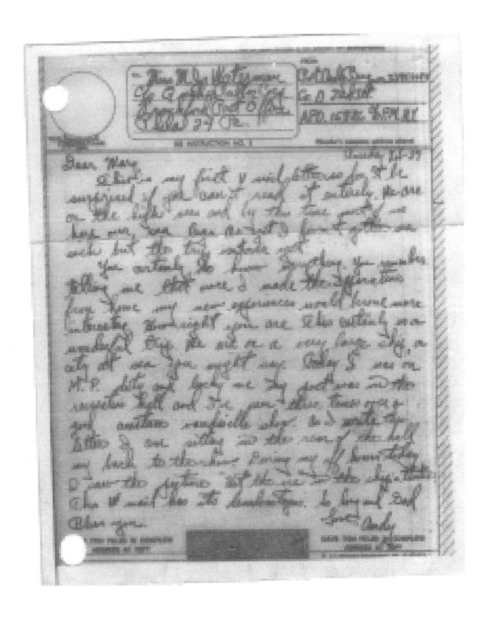

February 27, 1945

Dear Mary,

This is my first V mail letter so don't be surprised if you can't read it entirely. We are on the high seas and by this time most of us have our sea legs. As yet I haven't gotten sea sick but the trip isn't over yet.

You certainly do know everything. You remember telling me that once I made the separation from home my new experiences would become more interesting? How right you are. This certainly is a wonderful trip. We are on a very large ship, a city at sea you might say. Today I was on M.P. duty and lucky me my post was in the recreation hall and I've seen three times over a good amateur vaudeville show. As I write this letter I am sitting in the rear of the hall, my back to the show. During my off hours today I saw the picture "Hit the Ice" in the ship's theater. This V mail has its disadvantages. So long and God bless you.

Love, Andy

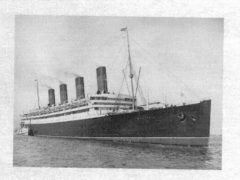

RMS Aquitania was a Cunard Line ocean liner designed by Leonard Peskett and built
by John Brown & Company in Clydebank,
Scotland. She sailed on her maiden voyage
to New York on 30 May 1914. Widely considered one of the most attractive ships
of her time, Aquitania earned the nickname "Ship Beautiful." During World War II
Aquitania sailed over 500,000 miles trans-
porting over 400,000 troops and was the
only liner to serve in both world wars.
Andy boarded the Aquitania at New York
Harbor on February 25, 1945. The ship carried nearly 10,000 soldiers, sleeping in
stacked bunks of 3 to 5 men. They made the
crossing in six days, arriving in Glasgow,
Scotland, on March 3.

Wednesday, February 28, 1945

Dear Mary,

If someone would only stop rocking my dream boat I could write a half legible letter. Yes in a way this is my dream boat, if only the dreams I made on this boat come true. This V-Mail was probably designed for fellows with little news. It seems that you must always sign off in the midst of something interesting. I'm at the show again tonight listening to some more British humor. The British really have a swell sense of humor. I think we will get along swell together.

I spent most of the day reading on deck. I recommend, "One World" by W. Wilbur and "Lend Lease" by Mr. Stillmius. They weren't as dry as I expected and they taught me a lot, but perhaps I am just too gullible. While on deck I saw things that led me to believe we weren't too far from land but that's only my idea. We are still a few days due. So long and God bless you.

Lots of love, Andy

Andy was assigned to L Company, 417th Regiment, 76th Infantry Division of the Third Army. The 76th was called "ONAWAY," the alert signal of the Chippewa Indians upon whose land the 76th trained in Wisconsin. The Division first arrived in Europe in January 1945 and began a 110 day, 400 mile push into Germany from Echternach, Luxembourg. The ONOWAY had success after success but not without significant casualties. A steady flow of replacement troops was critical to sustain the drive. In February 1945 alone, the company processed 973 reinforcements.

Wednesday, March 7, 1945

Dear Mary Jane,

Honest Injun it is ink. Golly for a while I thought I'd never write in ink again. Just found a fellow who has a traveling ink bottle and imposed on his generosity. Mary if you could possibly get ahold of one it certainly would be a help. The container seems to be made of hard rubber or some composition of Bakelite and has a leak proof screw top.

Haven't written to you for a few days. Well the last week has been very interesting. Since my last letter to you I have seen parts of three countries, Scotland, England and France. Scotland is a very beautiful land untouched by war as far as the landscape goes. England shows very definite signs of the horrors of war and France in one part that I saw was just leveled off. However, last night we saw the other side of town and it was pretty well intact. Really I am very lucky to get such an education for free. I bet I know what you are saying, "You and your education" …that's Jerry Cologna stuff.

Finally we have arrived at our initial depot. It is a tent city that reminds us of our bivouac back in the states except that here we have all the comforts of home. The tents are eight man pyramid type and we have a stove and cots in it. Last night we were issued sleeping bags so you see this is pretty much of alright.

Soon we will reach our intermediate depot and receive a new address, pay and a pass so that I can try out my high school French. Rumors! The grapevine has it that we may get mail here. I hope so. I could use a letter boost from home. The surprising thing about our bunch is the high morale for young fellows going into battle with what training we have had. Naturally, everyone is a wee bit excited and worried but you never saw a more cheerful and jolly bunch.

When we arrived [text cut from letter by censors] a British General came aboard and gave us the dope. He was very frank and that night I got a little more selfish in my prayers.

Andy recalled that the British General
who greeted their ship at the dock in
Glasgow said, "How fortunate you are to
arrive just in the nick of time to stem
the tide of Hitler's hoards."

Before, my prayers were general for the speedy victory and the safety and salvation of every soldier of any country anywhere, but that night I concentrated a little more on this G.I. Andy fellow. Thanks for your spiritual support in way of prayers and now maybe you could squeeze an extra one in for all the boys in our Co[1].

We realize our responsibility and are willing to stay that extra time and fight a little harder to ensure this lasting peace they talk about. The next time I see you folks I want it to be for good. This is my last patriotic duty in way of war. No more public wars for this fellow. Chow in five minutes. So long and God bless you.

Love, Andy

---

1   Company L, 417 Regiment, 76th Infantry division

Thursday, March 8, 1945

Dear Mary,

I am pretty fortunate. This is the second straight day I've had a chance to write to you. We're still at our initial depot. Today we were supposed to take a little training but did details instead. I was on a Headquarters detail. That's just a fancy name. I helped lay paths around the officers' mess hall. Tonight we are going to a show. It's quite a thrill, one of the famous firsts. My first show overseas. "Marriage by Mistake" is the name of the show. So far Army life oversees is not tough at all. Of course that is the Army life I have seen. So long and God bless you.

Love, Andy

P.S. Don't forget those prayers for us fellows.

Because of the critical need for reinforcements, Andy's basic training was cut from 17 to 13 weeks. After disembarking in Scotland, the troops were sent by train to Southampton, England, and by boat to Le Harve, France. It is likely that men from the 417th were initially sent to Camp Lucky Strike, the largest of the "Repo Depots" or replacement camps near the coast. All of the Repo Depots were named for cigarette brands to confuse the Germans and make the soldiers feel more at home. Camp Lucky Strike was a tent city with defined neighborhoods, hospitals, parks and entertainment centers. At its apex it housed 50,000 soldiers.

Saturday, March 10, 1945

Dear Mary,

Just finished writing a six page letter home so I'll have to make this letter a little shorter or the officers will find me something to do besides writing letters. Again last night we went to the show. See we even have nightlife overseas. The picture wasn't so good. "Marriage is a Private Affair" is all about divorce and well, it just wasn't right. The ending of the picture is O.K. because the stars make up and stay married but even that seemingly good ending couldn't repair the damage done to some kid's mind by the rest of the picture.

Yesterday I settled several arguments among the fellows by using that little Blue book you gave me before I left. It is from the Royle Machine Co. and contains much valuable information. Most of the arguments we have among ourselves are "which state is better." Well of course it's everyman for his own state. Your book has the population and square miles of each city and state and a list of the Presidents with some information about them. Thanks a lot for the book. It is very helpful to a world traveler like me.

This afternoon I was put on a detail. I don't know what we were supposed to be doing but after trying unsuccessfully to burn a pile of brush, we played football. It was the first time in a long while and it was fun.

No mail yet.

During one of his first days at the
initial depot, Andy was standing for
inspection when an Officer said to him,
"Soldier you haven't shaved today." To
this he replied, "Sir, I didn't shave
today or yesterday or the day before. I'm
only 18 years old, I've never shaved in my
life."

Yesterday's hike through town made me realize even more that there is a good reason for my being here. This is the kind of education you can't get any other way. It's the kind that makes you think and reason things out. Every time I think something out, I arrive at the same conclusion. This life doesn't mean much in a way and in a way it means everything. We are here to test whether we are worthy to enter the next world and what we do here determines whether or not we will obtain life everlasting in heaven. This life means everything to me because I know I must be good and fulfill my responsibilities in order to secure the everlasting happiness. It doesn't mean a thing to me because I assure myself I am fulfilling my duties and needn't worry about losing that for which I strive unless I slip. However, I still have that human instinct to live. To me all this makes sense. Well bye for now and God bless you.

Love from, Andy

Saturday, March 17, 1945

Dear Mary,

As yet I haven't gotten any mail so it's tough to write letters. About all I can say is that I'm feeling swell and suffering no hardship and that I want news from home.

Every day I become more convinced that the U.S. Army is the best organization of any kind. When I was still a civilian and was told about Army teamwork I believed it but not like I believe it now. Even the cooks do without certain foods so that the men on the front can have an extra share of it. They are a swell bunch. The Officers and men are the best of buddies. They work and fight together. No one likes to fight but they realize what is at stake and are doing an extra good job as the papers indicate. We are one happy, very big family with one end in sight.

Well bye for now, hoping to see you in three S's. Safe! Sound! Soon! God bless you.

Love, Andy

P.S. Please send candy

Sometime between March 11 and 15, Andy was sent by train to join the 417th near Trier, Germany. Their orders were to clear all enemy north of the Moselle River. The troops traveled in box cars called 40 & 8s because they could hold 40 men or 8 horses. From Trier, Andy was driven by jeep to the front. He recalls that the jeep trip took over four hours in the dead of night over badly shelled roads with mortars bullets flying. He was not sure he would survive to join the fight.

Andy carried an M1 Rifle, a trench knife and a 50 pound pack containing a sleeping bag, extra socks, writing materials and K - Rations. He also carried a bible with a metal cover which he kept in his breast-pocket over his heart.

On March 18th the 417th crossed the Moselle River near Mulheim. Other soldier accounts indicate that there was little initial resistance from German troops but that the woods were heavily mined. L Company pushed on towards the Rhine in the direction of Boppard and St. Goar clearing woods and towns as they went.

Saturday, March 24, 1945

Dear Mary,

Still no mail. Mary I wish you would let me know whether or not the type of letter I write reaches home completely[2] and whether it is the right kind. How does Mom take them? Maybe I'm too frank and talk too much. I don't want my letters to worry her and yet I don't want to mislead her with a line she won't believe anyhow. The only reason I tell of my activity is because we have it so good just now that I still have enough courage to write.

The thing I don't like about this business, and it is a very big business, is that usually there is very little time to write and you will find out they discourage writing. They claim that writing and thinking about home drives men crazy and tears down the morale of others. I guess I haven't seen enough action yet because I still like to write.

Mary, there are many occasions coming up like Mother's day, Dad's birthday, etc. Would you look after things for me? Maybe I can repay you in Belgian or French francs. No I am kidding. I'll repay you in good greenbacks if you set me straight. Thanks a lot.

Love, Andy

```
The 417th was encamped for several days
west of the Rhine River at the town of
St. Goar. Andy recalls being in the tower
of a castle on one side of the river and
exchanging fire with German troops in a
castle on the east side. On March 25th,
under cover of night, the 417th created
a diversion that simulated a river
crossing, while the actual crossing was
taking place just north at the town of
Boppard.
```

---

2   This is a reference to censorship. All outbound mail was reviewed and edited to remove references to locations, troop strength, actions or other military information that if intercepted by the enemy could put troops at risk.

Tuesday, March 27, 1945

Dear Mary,

At last, today Andy became his own self again. Yes, I came back home for the first time in over a month. Last night while lying on watch out on the line my Sargent crawled up and dumped 21 letters in my lap. Of course there was a remark to go with it but I was so thrilled I didn't hear him. Well, that was no time to start reading but I stuffed them in my already overflowing pockets and finally, this morning I read them all.

There were seven from Mary Jane plus an Easter greeting. I received letters No. 97, 98, 105, 107, 108, 109, 112. Oh, I forgot, the censor may cut those numbers out. Here goes again, ninety seven and eight, one hundred and five, seven, eight, nine and twelve. The last I received on the boat was number ninety-two so you see there are a few missing. None of the V-Mails were among the letters I received.

My writing today isn't so good for this town is being shelled as I write this letter.

```
Traveling through the north edge of
Frankfort the 417 found textile factories
and warehouses. Andy recalls "liberating"
underclothes from one warehouse only to
realize they were women's panties. The
men wore them anyway.
```

Your letters certainly are an inspiration to me. Now that I have received and read your letters I feel very much better about what will take place in the future. Those words of encouragement mean more to me than anything else anyone could give me. They mean the difference between life and death. That may sound funny but I'm here on a mission, a business trip and your advice is one of the main reasons I can go on without the fear most fellows have. Yes, I'm scared just like all of us but there is a difference between being scared and fearing something. That scared feeling is a natural reaction but fear goes much further. There is a little phrase in the Lord's Prayer, "Thy will be done." Every night in my prayers I repeat that a second time.

I'm sorry that I couldn't send you a card from Camp Shanks for your birthday but they had none. Here there is no way of relaying a greeting except by letter. Quite a bit has happened since my departure. Betty's wedding was a surprise to me. If I find time I will write and congratulate her. What is her new name now?

Your four proverbs on Relax, Remember, Rest and Relate seem to fill out my attitude fairly well. With every letter of yours I read I become more convinced that Andy is getting some very extra special grace to carry out his duties. I'll say goodbye for now and God bless you.

Love – lots of it, Andy

P.S. Please send candy

Wednesday, March 28, 1945

Dear Mary,

Only a couple days ago I was beginning to get the feeling that I was away from home but now that I have read all your letters, well here I am again in Burholme. Not only was I acquiring that alone feeling but I found myself trying to work up a hatred for the German people. That is the way the big shots want it but well you know me. I just can't get to hating anybody. I can get used to the idea that these people brought such grief on the rest of the world and I must treat them as enemy if I want the next generation of Bergners to live in peace in the U.S.A. That "A" is for America not Army.

You say that my ears should be ringing constantly because you are constantly thinking of me. Well the last few days they have been ringing just as much as my first day on the rifle range at J.T. Robinson. Yesterday we had rain while the sun was shining. Naturally I searched for the rainbow. Honestly, I found it. It was the first time I had seen it since I was a wee tot. Yes it was a beautiful sight for sore eyes. Just then things seemed to quiet down and we had all the indications of a peaceful world. That proves it won't be long now. So long and God bless you.

Love, Andy

P.S. Remember I like candy – Andy

After crossing the Rhine on March 28th, the 417th marched northeast in the direction of Berlin, clearing towns and encountering significant resistance. Over Easter weekend, March 29 and 30, at the town of Schmitten, north of Frankfurt am Maim, L Company took severe casualties and two platoons including Andy's were captured. Below is the story in his words, recorded in 2011.

Incident at Dorfwiel

It was east of the Rhine that we took the kick in
the pants. Unorganized resistance they called
it. After we crossed the river, Germans started
coming out of the forest waiving white flags
to surrender. But our commanders got word of a
battalion strength of German SS in the town of
Schmitten who were not going to surrender. They
decided to send a platoon, that is four tanks
and 30 soldiers, to each of four small towns
surrounding Schmitten. My platoon was sent to
Dorfweil. At Dorfweil our platoon was reduced
to three men. I was one … the rest had all been
captured. Here is what happened:

That evening in Dorfweil, I was standing guard
next to one of our tanks. The gunner in the tank
was an 18-year-old like me. He said, "I hope the
Germans come down this street because I've got
my cannon pointed and I'm going to let them have
it." When I was relieved of duty, I went to the
local butcher shop, which we had taken over as
our headquarters, to get some rest. I had just
laid down when the Germans did come down the
street making a huge noise and burning
buildings.

My commander said, "I need two volunteers - you
and you". I was the first you. Within minutes
he was hoisting me over a wall to run for
reinforcements. As I dropped to the other side
of the wall bullets were bouncing around me. I
crept on my knees 'til I found the door to an
underground cellar. I dropped into the cellar
and found a family of German civilians who had
already taken cover there. I used my gun and my
little bit of German to move them to the back of
the cellar and told them to be quiet.

A little later I heard German voices outside
saying, "Commenzie rout mit der hans holt,"
which meant - come out with your hands up. Then
the Germans marched the rest of my platoon away.
I stayed the rest of the night in the cellar.
The next morning I crept up to the third floor
of the house and saw our company commander
on the street looking for the platoon. I was
the only one left to go down and report to him
what had happened. I'm happy to say that we
recaptured most of the guys a few days later.

Thursday, April 5, 1945

Dear Mary,

It has been quite a while since my last letter to you. In that time we have been very busy. It seems a lot of people want this war to end in a hurry and I suppose our outfit is the only one in on it because our feet are sore and our eyes hang heavy. I'm only kidding about our outfit being the only ones doing anything but it is a big job and soon we will all get the rest we need.

Outside of being tired and weary, I am still in the same fine health and high spirits as when I left you. Yes, I remember everything you tell me in your letters. Maybe not word for word but the impression lingers and that is what keeps me going and keeps me alert while I am going. I think I still remember exactly what Mr. Bremer told me that day. He was right about everything except, "the infantry doesn't ride." So long and God bless you.

Love, Andy

The 417th continued their swift but bloody march eastward, liberating the captured American platoons at Arnsbach and facing heavy fighting at the town of Helsa, where the Germans tried unsuccessfully to protect an ordinance supply facility and their escape route to the north. On April 5 the 417th crossed the Werra River, later crossing the Gera and Saale Rivers, clearing town after town of German resistance and sending thousands of surrendered or captured Germans to the prisoner cages.

Andy recalled that his unit was moving too fast even to stop and process the German POWs. They just pointed to the west and told them to keep walking and surrender to the next Americans they found.

Friday, April 13, 1945

Dear Mary,

By this time it is probably a novelty to receive a letter from Europe written by some guy called Andy. I'm sorry about that but there is good reason for it. In a very short while now the end of this holocaust will come and with it more letters. I started addressing this form on Tuesday and that is as far as I got. Since Tuesday there hasn't been anything really exciting happen to us except that we collected a few more blisters.

The last two days I've tended fairly well to the needs of my stomach. It was in bad shape. K rations become tiresome and the cake, eggs and other items of food furnished by the German civilians are mighty tasty and have restored my appetite, you know my appetite. On Tuesday I received several letters from you and was pleased to learn that Carl Grunwald is serving in the same Army as I am. So long and God bless you.

Love, Andy

```
'On April 14, the 417th swept into the
town of Zeitz to relieve the 304th who
been battling for a full day against an
entrenched German force. Zeitz housed
a German Officer Candidate School
whose Commander had vowed never to be
taken. On the 15th the Americans agreed
to a temporary truce to allow for the
evacuation of German wounded, but when the
Germans broke the truce the 417th launched
an all-out assault on the school, shelling
it until the white flag of surrender
appeared out of the rubble. Later that
day Andy's unit liberated a concentration
camp, freeing 250 Russian POWs and 1,000
French slave laborers. In addition to the
notorious extermination camps, the Nazi
regime maintained nearly 1,500 forced
labor camps, populated by citizens from
many countries.
```

Friday, April 20, 1945

Dear Mary,

Yesterday we had mail call twice. In the morning I received your letter number one twenty three. In the afternoon, letter number one thirty seven written April 4 arrived. Letter one thirty seven contained the information I have been waiting for. If I used my head for a little more than a helmet holder I would have realized that the letters I have been writing aren't helping my folks any. They have it so much tougher than I do for my hardship is mostly physical. Of course now I am very confused about many things but being a doughboy it is my right and duty to bitch and complain about everything unpleasant.

You folks back home, however, haven't the physical strain to distract your mind from what that fellow in Germany is doing right now so you just worry and worry some more. Unlike us you can't complain because there is no one to blame, no one to complain to. And in the past week or so, it has been proved that mental strain is much tougher than what I am going through. The sudden death of F.D.R.[3] is what I am thinking of. He was only 63 but probably could have been 83 or 93 if he was just an ordinary laborer. I'm not a doctor, but if he died of a cerebral hemorrhage, maybe it was from too much worry.

The reason my letters seem so discouraging is because there is nothing else to write about. We haven't done anything until yesterday except carry on the war. Yes, yesterday for the first time since last summer I played ball. An American baseball game on a German athletic field.

I always figured it was right to keep home on your mind to give you a worthwhile purpose for life, but some of my more recent spots have changed my mind. Now that the sun is shining and it is a beautiful warm spring day my thoughts of home are refreshing but there are many situations here also where if you did think of home you would go crazy and become easy prey. If all this sounds silly and confusing, just remember this fellow is pretty tired and confused himself. Maybe wars aren't for eighteen year old brains. Anyway, I do promise that from now on I will confide in you and tell you the things I must tell someone but shouldn't

---

3   President Franklin Delano Roosevelt died April 12, 1945, of a cerebral hemorrhage.

write home. I just gotta do what's right by you and the folks owing you so much that I can never, ever repay.

About all the birthday's back home. Got paid 510 Marks last week and now am working on a $50 money order home. So you see, money here is no good to a fellow in this outfit. If you will let me know just how much I'm in the red with you, next payday I could send a money order and get a clean slate again. Still no packages as yet but it shouldn't be long now. There isn't anything that I can use because we can't carry much with us. Well thanks for everything you are doing to keep me informed and try to understand how thoroughly confused all this has me right now. So long and God bless you. See you in three S's.

Love, Andy

P.S. Please send some candy

```
The 417th crossed the Mulde River on
April 16 and set up a defensive position
about 5 kilometers east of the German
occupied city of Chemnitz. There they
received a change of orders. Rather
than proceeding to Berlin, they were
to wait for the Russian army that was
rapidly advancing from the east and pinch
Hitler off between them. After a month
of unrelenting marching, dubbed the Rat
Race, by the 76th, this period of relative
calm was both a welcome relief and a
frustrating delay. Despite the relaxation
and entertainments described in Andy's
letters, the troops were still on alert,
conducting combat patrols, engaged in
periodic skirmishes and taking German
prisoners.

On April 20, 1945, Hitler's 56th birthday,
the 76th Regiment honored him by firing 56
mortar rounds into the German SS Barracks
in Chemnitz.
```

Saturday, April 21, 1945

Dear Mary,

Two more letters from you yesterday, one thirty one and one thirty three. The mail is really coming in now. Every day I receive five or six letters. Yesterday, after writing to you I succeeded in writing a cheery letter home for a change. This will continue as long as I am able.

Lately we in Germany have been enjoying the same bright warm sunshine and the same new budding and blossoming vegetation you folks back home do. Yesterday we all had spring fever for there was no ball game for our platoon. We just laid on the warm green grass sniffing in its new fragrance. The more ambitious fellows took pictures of their sleeping buddies, etc. Yes they even wasted a little of the film on me. I'm glad to hear Bill Ryder finally got back home and came to visit Quaker. It certainly makes me feel good to hear that all my lady friends still ask for me. Maybe the three years working after school in the fruit store[4] was worthwhile. Mrs. Straub also has a son in the service. Yes, I have felt that someone is guiding me to the right place at the right time. Bye for now or (auf wiedersehen). God bless you.

Love from your careful, Andy

---

4   Charles Mayers Produce Market in downtown Burholme

Sunday, April 22, 1945

Dear Mary,

Yes we're still taking it easy and leading the life of a king. Last night we went to a very exclusive theater, the Astoria, and took in the picture show, "Strange Affair." It was a swell picture. The Germans even enjoyed attending the shows at the Astoria at one time. Now the Yanks use it to take care of their spiritual and recreational needs. This morning Mass was held in the theater.

Just a short while ago I enjoyed my first shower in six weeks. It was nice and hot and we could stay in it as long as we wanted. If you have any idea what a shower fan I was back home you can understand what a treat that was for me. This seems to be sort of a warm clearing in this part of my life. Of course the real clearing will not come until I come home but this sure is a help.

This is so like garrison life. Tomorrow we are having an all - out inspection so I must clean my rifle this afternoon in order to go to the show tonight. Well bye for a while and God bless you.

Love from your careful, Andy

Tuesday, April 24, 1945

Dear Mary,

Tomorrow begins the Frisco Conference. Let's hope that's the beginning of Japan's end. Joe should also be home tomorrow from all the latest reports. If only he can get another good deal[5] and hang around the states until final and complete victory. Yesterday I was very well taken care of, five letters from you. Letter #141 contained a picture of Mary Jane in her liberty bell dress. It sure is a swell dress and a swell picture and a sweller girl.

You certainly are the cause of all my good fortune. You buy a chance for me and I win. That proves something. No. 144 must be my lucky number. It was my old time card number at Quaker. The more I think of winning that $15.00, the more convinced I am that my worries are over, that the news on my side cannot be disappointing. God bless you and I will write tomorrow from our new home.

Love, Andy

The Frisco Conference refers to the United Nations Charter Conference, which was held in San Francisco from April 25 to June 26, 1945. The conference, coming at the close of World War II, was sponsored by the major Allied powers - the United States, Great Britain, China, and Russia - with delegates from 46 other countries participating. The goal of the conference was to approve a charter for an international peace - keeping entity in the hope that future global conflict might be avoided. After just two months, the charter was approved and signed by 50 of the 51 original member nations (Poland, absent from the conference, signed later). It took effect on October 24, 1945. (Source - Minnesota Historical Society)

---

5   Andy's brother Joe was accepted into Marine officer candidate school at Colgate College in Pennsylvania, keeping him stateside for the duration of the war.

Wednesday, April 25, 1945

Dear Mary,

It's about 2 in the afternoon and the sun has just decided to stay out for the rest of the day. We are in the field today and the sun just makes me want to lay down in the cool green grass and sleep for the duration. Yes, about 12 or 15 years ago to vacation in Germany would have been the best vacation possible. I have been convinced of that after seeing as much of this country as possible in the last few weeks during the best season of the year. Everything is so green. A million shades of green anyway you look. Cool breezes and bright sunshine are giving me the worst case of spring fever I ever had. Maybe the lack of exercise recently is also helping this spring fever.

Yesterday two letters from Mary Jane, 140 and 145. Were you trying to rub it in putting a "Join the U.S. Marines" seal on the envelope? Just for that I think I will join the Marines for a few years after the war. This morning there was four letters from you. Three of them, 117, 119 and 121 were written to A.P.O. 15786 so you can see all the back mail is finally getting to me.

In letter 117 you say I must be getting highbrow from all the educating books I read coming over here on the Aquitania. Well, they were the last reading I have done except for news. I am expecting the arrival of the Readers Digest so that I can learn how to read all over again. Your guardian angel seems to be working overtime lately. Receiving mail almost every day is almost miraculous with the conditions now. Yes, I certainly have been fortunate. Thanks again and again and again for now. Well the Major[6] is on his way on a tour of inspection so I'll say Auf Wiedersehen until tomorrow and God bless you.

Love from your lucky, Andy

---

6 Major General William R. Schmidt, division commander

Sunday, April 29, 1945

Dear Mary,

From the sound of most of your five letters received today, you seem to doubt that I'm O.K. You want to know if I am getting enough rest. Right now yes! Plenty. And now that it is over it won't harm you to know that there were times when I was writing very little or not writing at all that we went three days and nights without any rest. This advance was very rapid and maybe we would get 12 or 15 hours of sleep a week and nothing but K rations to eat and whatever else we could get from the German civilians.

Sometimes we wouldn't stop for the night and when we did there was always security or guard duty to keep you from resting. One morning we pulled out at 2:45 a.m. with about 45 minutes sleep that night. Well the majority of fellows were falling asleep walking along the roads. Believe me, that is possible. About an hour later we ran into trouble that woke everyone up in a hurry. You wanted to know, but everything is all right now and has been for some time.

That's the Army for you. One day we work real hard and the next you don't do a thing. Well I must sign off now. So long and God bless you.

Love, Andy

Monday, April 30, 1945

Dear Mary,

Well here I am again and maybe this time without...Oh Oh (pause). Gosh some brainless idiot just fired his rifle. Some fellows think we have no nerves. Here we are in our holes[7] in defense against the enemy and some joker scares us half to death just for the devil of it. As I was trying to say, maybe I could write a letter without being interrupted but I guess not. From you two letters of today I see that everyone is taking care of me as far as sweets go. A box of candy from Russ and Nell and 25 chocolate bars from Mr. Wharton. Golly that sounds good. Honestly there isn't anything else I need or can use.

Don't let the fact that we are in foxholes worry you. Everything is OK and this is just for added protection, but any shots being fired make us wonder. Well the word just came down that we will have a rifle inspection so again I must close and say God bless you.

Love from lucky, Andy

---

7 The 417th is still defending their position from fox holes 5 kilometers west of Chemnitz.

Wednesday, May 3, 1945

Dear Mary,

We have been having a wide variety of weather the last few days, rain, snow and hail. Does that sound like good May weather? We don't like it either but any kind or variety of weather is better than enemy opposition. Intel reports all German resistance has ceased and Hitler is Kaput[8]. That's good and now all we do is sweat and hope. The Pacific war is still long from over. You know, I think I'd rather be sent overseas to the U.S. than any other place. Maybe your wishes, hopes and prayers can help. You seem to give special grace to everything that happens to me. Bye for now and God bless you.

Love from, Andy

---

8   Adolph Hitler committed suicide on April 30, 1945.

Friday, May 4, 1945

Dear Mary,

If you folks are still following "Old Blood and Guts" to trace Andy please stop. There have been some changes made here and General Patton fights alone now. [9] The Bergner / Patton conformation came a long way and finally the Chief decided he could get along without me. Tried to tell you before of the change but it was probably cut out for the next day we were told not to. Sorry that I can't give you more dope now. Now I must sign off and try to get some sleep for tonight we may have a job.

Love from your careful, Andy

---

9   On April 27, 1945, command of the 76th Infantry was transferred from General George Patton's 3rd Army to the 1st Army under the command of General Omar Bradley.

Tuesday, May 8, 1945

VE + One

Dear Mary,

By this time you folks have learned that now Japan stands alone as a menace to democracy. Again "I told you so." In yesterday's letter to you I expressed my belief that something good and something big was happening back home. Well, as usual I was right. Something good and big did happen though not exactly back home. I still want that report on how folks reacted yesterday in the U.S. In a letter home I tried to tell the folks how things went over here. The main concern now is when and what. When will we get home and what will become of us now. The Pacific war needs men, darn it. The Pacific war is what put the damper on the celebrations here.

Now we are living the soft life with nothing to do except eat, sleep and write. Soon we will be issued clean clothes and extra clothes and again go in a little more for glamour. The German people don't think much of the American Army because of their appearance and seeming lack of discipline. Now that the big job is over we will concentrate more on these things. Last night saw the show "Roughly Speaking" and enjoyed it very much. In it, Jack Carson made the statement, "home is a feeling not a place." That is why I have been home all this while although thousands of miles from 7427.

Maybe if it should be a while before we leave here I can take part in some sort of educational program to keep me out of trouble and on the ball for my schooling later on. The Army may change some men's way of thinking but I haven't given up my chemistry idea yet. Bye for now and God bless you.

Love, Andy

Wednesday, May 9, 1945

VE + Two and a beautiful May day at last

Dear Mary,

As I was lying on my back in this tall, cool, green grass under the semi - shade of the large pines in this clean looking German wooded area, one begins to realize what Victory Europe really means. At first the official report of the long overdue, much awaited armistice was received with a stun of wonderment. We sort of gave a sigh and inwardly said, "now what." I do believe that not one of us linemen realized what it meant to him individually and I confess it took me until today to reach a decision.

It means that once again we can settle comfortably down and rest. You can, if you want, go to sleep in this glorious spring atmosphere. You can sleep a sleep of peace not having constant fear in your mind, or your buddies safety on your conscience. Now at last you have time for your eyes and mind to just wander and observe things other than the military. You can notice how clean these woods are and even question why? Eighty million people in a space about the size of Texas must be very conservative and they are. There isn't a twig of loose wood around. Every available stick is utilized and people go maybe a mile before they cut a tree. Even the simple farmer can amaze you. His way of working seems old fashioned for you have been used to the rapid production method with tractors, etc. This farmer uses a team of horses and a hand plow.

Things are so peaceful and quiet but you still can't quite realize that your safety is assured. The bright sun, the cool breezes humming through the pine and the whistling of the birds; all these signs of spring, even the farmer's horses seem to be in love, they so cheerfully do their chore; bring you to realize how lucky you are to witness such a special and beautiful countryside today when only a very short while ago things were so different. It's something like this that lets you know just how small you are. You realize you are a little cog in one of the millions of watches of this earth, with Almighty God as the watchmaker. Surely, this is a day of thanksgiving and what better way is there to give thanks to God than by realizing that your every action should be for his honor and glory.

Maybe all this sounds like a sermon but it is the way I look at things. It is the way my folks have taught me to look at things and it is the way I can help keep myself straight and out of trouble in this life. Thanks very much to you and your mother for all your prayers. They pulled us through in fine shape.

Love from a well satisfied friend, Andy

P.S. Don't forget and give me the dope on the Victory Celebration of the B W Corp., or has it been postponed until the three absent Bs return?

```
Victory in Europe Day - or VE Day, is a public
holiday celebrated on May 8 to mark the date
when the World War II Allies formally accepted
the unconditional surrender of the armed
forces of Nazi Germany and the end of Adolf
Hitler's Third Reich, thus ending the war in
Europe. However, the act of military surrender
was signed on May 7, 1945 in Reims, France, so
troops in the field considered that day to be
VE day.
```

Saturday, May 12, 1945

Dear Mary,

Well I stood guard all night from 2 o'clock on and when I tried to sleep this morning you wouldn't let me. I don't mind. After I had been sleeping maybe 30 minutes the platoon runner woke me up to go down stairs and carry my mail up. Guess he figured I should carry the four packages myself. Yes, today four of the packages arrived. Two from Mary and two from Mom. One of your packages contained the leak proof, traveling inkwell. Thanks a lot Mary, it's just the thing I wanted. The rest of the contents of both packages is much appreciated by the squad. All these sweets will keep us happy for a while.

Now we are on occupational guard duty. That's a fancy name and no one knows just how long this deal will last. It is a good deal and as much as I want to get home in a hurry please pray that this deal keeps me here for several months. It is probably the safest thing as long as the Japs still fight. Well bye for now and God bless.

Love from your very lucky, Andy

Sunday, May 13, 1945

Dear Mary,

Andy is a well satisfied fellow today. The mail man, who knows him very well by now continued his generosity and even increased it a little. About 20 letters and a package is the score for today. The package contained some very badly needed stationary; the envelopes are already in use. The candy is "kaput" and the olives, crackers and other delicacies are safely tucked away for that hungrier moment. Five packages in two days makes me boss around here.

Today the boys seem to have made some new connections with our Russky friends because they are celebrating more vigorously the recent victory. I just finished putting a quiet one to bed now I hear the noisy trouble maker types downstairs. As I told Mom, these boys deserve their fun, I know, I was with them. I hope I never see fun in the same things, the idea doesn't particularly appeal to me. I'm getting tired and must sleep. Again so long and God bless you.

Love from your, Andy

Tuesday, May 15, 1945

Dear Mary,

Warner Grose is right. Some of these German girls are rather attractive but to speak to them costs sixty five dollars in fines. I only draw thirty dollars a month so I can't afford to talk to Germans except in the line of duty.

Yes, I have had the chance to experience that fear you told me about. Usually when it was time to really fear, too much was happening and I sort of unknowingly defied all opposition. Now that it is all over I'm sure that I didn't realize the danger when I acted almost foolishly. I find I was more afraid of things that weren't real or were untrue.

Yes, I received all the pictures that have been sent me. The latest were pictures taken while Joe was at home. Perhaps I should be jealous of that big handsome Marine who is hanging on to that gorgeous little lady with the big smile. So you feel we will soon be chattering in person. I hope so. Many people feel that the Japanese war will end soon. I also hope they are right but they who say that don't know what war is.

I am glad you are getting mail from Fritz because the mail service between here and India isn't so good. The letters must go through New York and it takes a long time. If things turn out as Blanche and I want, you will see Fritz before long.

You folks must have been very much confused on VE Day but you were no more confused than we were. We were told that the war was over and 20 minutes later the platoon was called out to stop a regt. of Jerries who were pushing our way. I'll sign off for now. So long and God bless you.

Love from your, Andy

Thursday, May 17, 1945

Germany

Dear Mary,

Here I am trying my luck at the typewriter again. If I don't make to many mistakes this letter should be easier for you to read. Just now I am using the hunt and peck system of typing but maybe someday I'll learn the right way.

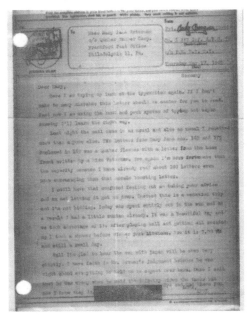

Last night the mail came in as usual and also I received more than anyone else. Two letters from Mary Jane nos. 169 and 175. Enclosed in 169 was a Quaker Flash with a letter from the home front written by a Miss Waterman. Here again I am more fortunate than the majority because I have already read about 100 letters even more encouraging than that morale boosting letter.

I still have that confused feeling but am taking your advice and not letting it get me down. Instead, this is a vacation trip and I'm not kidding. Today was spent entirely out in the sun and as a result I have a little suntan already. It was a beautiful day and we took advantage of it. After playing ball and getting all sweated up, I took a shower before dinner just like home. Now it is 7:00 PM and still a swell day.

Well I'm glad to hear the war in Japan will be over shortly. I have confidence in Mr. Bremer's judgment because he was right about everything he told me to expect over here. Once I said he was wrong that the infantry rides in tanks but now I know that they do. Bye and God bless you.

Love, Andy

Saturday, May 19, 1945

Dear Mary,

Tonight I am a very tired and hoarse G.I. We just returned from a ball game which our team lost 3 to 1. I really enjoyed playing and enjoyed talking it up and now I must suffer with a slight sore throat. Did I tell you that the E.T.O[10]. G.I.s are going to school while awaiting shipment? Today I filled in my application and I hope you'll agree that the courses I have chosen, although not in the line of my intended vocation, will do their intended job. I've got a lot of "intended" in there. Maybe soon we can have reality and fact instead of intentions and hopes. My courses were, Business Law, Salesmanship, Bookkeeping and Accounting. Does that sound at all worthwhile?

Today I received your letter of May 11th. Eight days is good time for a letter. Here's a request Mary. There is a shortage of good softballs over here. Could you please get hold of a good one and get it to me snell[11] like. Thanks a lot. Well this G.I. is ready to retire.

Love from your thankful, Andy

---

10 European Theater of Operations

11 Andy's attempt at *schnell*, the German word for fast.

Monday, May 21, 1945

First day of summer

Dear Mary,

Everything seemed to go wrong today until mail call. You wouldn't let me go to bed in a dejected mood. Along with another wave of three packages came your letters #177 and #179 and letters from Joe, Mrs. Folhenson, Grace and Rosemarie. The gang is now eating and drinking what I received today in the packages while I sit down and write these letters. It's the truth. I would rather write than eat. Two of the packages were from Mom and one from the Watermans. In your package along with Whitman's chocolates were Oh Henry bars and rum and butter toffee. Is there significance to the Oh! Henry (Oh! Andy) bars? In the packages from home was fruit cake, cocoa, candy, lobster, fruit extract and sugar. As yet I haven't looked at the articles on the Peace Conference but in the morning I will have time.

Your loving, lucky, thankful friend, Andy

Wednesday, May 23, 1945

Dear Mary,

Last night I received letter #180. I hope it never reaches the 200 mark. Every day I become more confident of going home. Today I have 20 points toward my discharge instead of 15 because they gave me another battle star. Those 20 points are as good as 0 but all the rumors now are good rumors.

Well tonight our team won its first ball game. The score was 8 to 1 so maybe now we'll start rolling. Extra! Flash! Etc.! This evening for dessert we had the best chocolate ice cream I tasted since I have been here. Of course it was the first ice cream seen in Europe for six years but it was the best. Guten Nacht and God bless you.

Love from your lucky, Andy

The Advanced Service Rating Score was the system that the U.S. Army used at the end of World War II in Europe to determine which soldiers were eligible to be sent back to the United States for discharge from military service. The principle was that those that fought the longest and hardest should be discharged first. An enlisted man needed a score of 85pts to be considered for the demobilization. The scores were determined as follows for each:
Month in service = 1 pt
Month in service overseas = 1 pt
Combat award (including battle stars) = 5 pts
Dependant child under 18 = 12 pts

Sunday, May 27, 1945

Zeulenroda

Dear Mary,

Does that word at the top right hand corner confuse you?
Well that is the name of this town. We moved here yesterday to
train for two weeks just to keep us busy. Today the schedule was
given to us. We must arise at 600 hours for an eight hour training
schedule. We will have off Saturday afternoon and Sunday. Most
of the training consists of athletics and P.T. with a little tactics
with tanks here and there. This training is just to improve our
alertness and discipline and to keep us busy until we are ready for
shipment. According to the latest rumors, I may celebrate my 19th
birthday in the U.S.A. Don't be alarmed or overjoyed about 1st
Army news any more for I am now in the 9th. Well I must get on
the ball and clean my rifle in order to pass inspection. So long and
God bless you.

Love from your, Andy

Sunday, May 27, 1945

Dear Folks,

Ever since the censorship has been lifted I wanted to let you in on a few secrets of the past. Now that the War is over and you know I am safe, you probably don't care about how I got here but I know Dad and this is for his benefit. It would be too much for one night or one letter so I'll continue tonight until I tire and resume tomorrow where I left off.

It was the 25th of February when the band played "Over There" as we took our last train ride in the States from Camp Shanks to the piers in New York. The time was 11 P.M. and we didn't know what pier or street or anything. You can realize the confusion caused by the crowded conditions the first night on shipboard. I do remember that the Red Cross was on hand with coffee, doughnuts and chocolate bars. I also remember much sweating was done that night.

We arose the next morning in time to see the Big Lady with the torch standing in the harbor. Try to imagine my thoughts for those ten minutes. Sweat, cold chills and enough goose pimples for a Thanksgiving Dinner were only a small part of my reaction. One thought was, "Lady, hope to see you soon again". Mom, I will kiss the soil first thing on debarking in the States again.

The trip was very pleasant, restful and uneventful. Fair weather and bright sunshine followed the good ship "Aquatania" the entire distance. The ship and the weather were fine but the chow was worthless. The chow was probably the cause of many cases of seasickness on board. No, I didn't get stricken. The menu called for two meals a day, the evening meal featuring the same baloney, always white hard boiled eggs and oatmeal for breakfast. To keep myself out of crap games I read two books during the voyage. "One World" furnished by Hank and Erna and, "Lease Lend" purchased at Camp Shanks.

The trip lasted for seven days for on March 3rd we landed near Glasgow, Scotland. The harbor and surrounding terrain was the most impressive sight I have ever seen. Battleships, aircraft carriers and submarines were greatly outnumbered by Henry J's version of the cargo vessels.

The harbor was huge but larger still were the green hills and snow - capped peaks in the background. We stayed on the harbor overnight so that's where I'll leave you tonight.

Bye now, Andy

Wednesday, May 30, 1945

Memorial Day

Dear Mary,

Today, Memorial Day was a very good day for Andy. Well, why shouldn't it be, almost every day is a good day for me thanks to all the prayers you folks are saying for me.

At 11:45 this morning the Company, all the companies in fact, fell out for a retreat formation in honor of all our buddies who will never return to the states. Many things flashed through my mind as I presented arms. It seemed such a shame that some boys died so late in the game, fighting against an Army that claim now they didn't want to fight. Why did that boy have to die maybe at the same time his wife was bringing a child into the world? And the kid that was so much afraid of the least little noise why did he stop a slug? Hope this doesn't sound too alarming that I am questioning God's justice. I'm not. But I am confused as I have been ever since my arrival here. Now I realize how young mentally I am. Should I try to figure this all out and if so should I be able to with my wisdom of 18 years?

Well at 1630 or 4:30 P.M. my faith in God was completely assured at a Requiem Mass in memory of these same buddies. Someone had to go and God's justice spared me to my folks and to you Mary, so that is proof of how deserving the B - W Corporation is. Sorry to disappoint you Mary but I'm not on the way home. Well so long and God bless you.

Love from your confused but lucky, Andy

Response to Andy's Memorial Day Letter
June 8, 1945 - # 204

Now Andy,

You are finding out daily no doubt, more mysteries of life –
more questioning thoughts enter your mind than you had ever
dreamed would be yours. However, just as I told you – my belief
is that your life is planned the day you enter the world. What is
to be will be – and it is only through the power of your faith – the
courage of your heart – and your will to do what is right – that
keeps you going when the road is rough – when the lights grow
dim – when the ice on the Lake of Contentment becomes too thin
for the skaters – that is where you prove what you are made of.
Don't wonder about the other fellow – don't question why he had
to suffer – or had to be the target when targets were popular in
your part of the world. Maybe those particular lives…had served
their purpose…their job was done.

Your present experiences make you wonder and think about
essentials now that you have more intimately faced the fact of
being, of life, death, present and future. But the answers cannot
be given by our own wisdom – they are only given by revelation –
that revelation most people find in God alone. You have no reason
to doubt, no reason to become confused. Remember, you are on a
trip – during your trip there are certain obligations to humanity –
certain obligations to your Country – to your Flag – and to your
loved ones at home. By doing YOUR share you are doing the
share of your Mother and Dad and my Mother who are beyond
the years of those who are wanted to serve. You are also doing the
share of Madge and Kate and I who are trying to do a certain part
along with taking care of our dear parents. However, yours is a
heavy burden – yours requires stamina and ability – but yours will
pay the biggest dividends in the end – that feeling that comes only
when you know deep down inside of you that YOU were the only
one responsible for the job YOU did.

Keep up your spirits – it is a big game and it calls for big
people and your Mary Jane knows that you will see the job to the
end and when you get back I'll even let you win one argument.
What more can you ask for?

MJ

Thursday, May 31, 1945

Dear Mary,

    I'm not sure I told you that I received $4.80 a month raise. Yes, now I have a total pay of $74.80. That's a lot of money for a P.F.C. We are the best paid Army in the world. What made me think of this was tomorrow is payday in U.S. money so what does that mean to us. Let me set you straight on the pay if you don't already know. Base pay for a P.F.C. is 54 dollars. Twenty percent for oversees pay is $10.80 more and combat pay is $10 more. That's where the $74.80 comes from.

Love from your, Andy

PFC Davis, Andy and Sgt. James Baude, near Reuth Germany

Saturday, June 2, 1945

Dear Mary,

One year ago today I sweated out my graduation exercises from Northeast Catholic High School. Before this date comes around again, one year from today, I will be a student again. Well, anyway that's something to hope and pray for. Funny thing, I never cared too much for school but now I'm sure I could make a go of it. Yes, it will be awfully tough for me but maybe this experience was necessary to make me realize that I must work and fight very hard for those things I dream of.

Tonight I must thank you and Mom and Mom Waterman for another package received. It was sent March 10th. The cookies, although a little crumbled, were good with the chocolate ice cream we had this evening.

May I quote Joe from his letter of today, "Mary Jane has been more than a friend of yours, she has been keeping both Fritz and I along with the rest of the family adequately supplied with everything, especially Morale. She's one in a million, take it from me". Well I wish to correct him slightly. You're one in one hundred thirty - one million. Thanks again and God bless you.

Love from your grateful, Andy

Thursday, June 7, 1945

D Day + 366[12]

Dear Mary,

This letter is very important. It is my first to you in about four days. The last few days there has been just too much entertainment here that I have neglected all else. I received five letters from you since my last report to you. They are Nos. 191, 193, 194, 195 and 196. Also since my last letter I received six more packages, two from Mom, one from Mary (thanks again) one from Madge, one from Kate and one from the Metz's. As things stand now I have a duffel bag full of goodies again and we are to move out on Saturday to a new location. This time it is a town called Reichenbach and an assignment guarding prisoners. The sand you send from Ocean City was very much appreciated by some fellows whose home is in N.J. They could at least finger the soil of their native state.

Near Pollnitz with PFC. Bill Cherry and Sgt. James Baude. Andy is on the right.

---

12   D Day is the term used to describe the Allied invasion at Normandy Beach on June 6, 1944.

Mr. Bremer's statement about the Japanese war sounds much too good to be true. The fellows give me the horselaff on that one. Golly, if that did come about we may be in the States at the time and could really give thanks to God as it should be done.

There are quite a few cameras in the Company. Yesterday D + 365, a holiday for us, I borrowed one and took some snaps. We were swimming and there are some of Andy in his trunks so you can see he is still healthy. I did lose quite a bit of weight while moving so rapidly with not much food, but now am gaining it all back and then some. Maybe you want me to explain all this entertainment? Well, I am a member of the Company ball team. We play about three times a week. Every night there is a movie, USO show, musical, symphony or something. Yesterday it was swimming and an honest to goodness circus, the best I have ever seen.

Today along with 5 other fellows I took training in the operation and use of the U.S. Army 300 Field Radio. Tomorrow we will go on a road guard. Just think, all alone with a radio, rations, writing materials and a book for the whole day. Well, I'll write again tomorrow. Bye for now and God bless you.

Lots of love from your very lucky, Andy

Friday, June 8, 1945

Dear Folks,

I'm very pleased to report still no let - up in the package situation. Yes, another today, a total of eight for this week. When we move out tomorrow I'll have an extra load but I don't mind that kind of load.

Unloading boats for the Rhine Crossing

Also tonight I received the June issue of the Reader's Digest. Read one article on the Rhine Crossing. It says our Third Army crossed silently. That's true we did, however, some good deception was used. Here is the part I (our Platoon) played in the Rhine Battle:

Out of a whole division, just one platoon, the platoon I happen to be in (the 3rd of L Co. 417 Inf.) occupied the town of St. Goar. Two crossings were made two successive nights – the first night our platoon with much artillery backing us up put up a very terrific sham battle downstream. The second night the 89th Division crossed at St. Goar as we lay silently in support. We didn't fire a shot – the surprise worked. That same night we drew back reformed with our battalion and crossed the next day on a pontoon bridge that the 87th Division had completed already.

The laughable part was the first night of the sham battle. The Engineers again did the job that night. All we did – we fired just as fast as we could while the Engineers laid down a terrific smoke screen – raced trucks up and down the street – screeched brakes – picked boats up and let them fall – squirted hoses on boats and cussed. You'd hear a boat drop and someone would yell, "God damn this #($'%&_boat". It sounded just like a real crossing and just a mile or so away, without a sound, a whole regiment got across before being discovered. I know that sounds like kid stuff but we are only kids, and besides it worked.

It was East of the Rhine that we took the kick in the pants. Unorganized resistance they called it – yet if you've ever heard of the towns, Schmitten or Dorfweil about 20 miles from Frankfurt on the Maine you'd change your mind. At Dorfweil, our platoon was reduced to three men. I was one and the rest had all been captured. I believe I told you then of my charmed life. Well, that wasn't true but your prayers were.

Pontoon Bridge over the Rhine

Then there was another little skirmish in the woods, "Go get em, only a couple snipers." "Don't let them stop you." Those couple snipers polished off a good part of our squad. We resumed the attack with four men in the squad. That was the day I resigned very suddenly as B.A.R.[13] man so I could get a wounded man to safety. You gotta help one another out in a spot like that.

---

13   BAR refers to the Browning Automatic Rifle, an early machine gun, heavier than an MI and able to shoot 30 round magazines. It could be fired from the hip, call walking fire, but was most frequently used in a stationary position with a tripod.

Mom, I apologize, I know you don't want to hear this kind of stuff. Maybe Dad doesn't either but I want to tell it to you once and forget it forever. The War is over a month already. Soon I'll be home and we can do things up right. I expect to be home when the Japanese surrender. Today we received the news of 62,000 Jap Soldiers surrendering. Take it for what it is worth.

Your loving son, Andy

P.S. Dad you said don't be tough on the old folks and young kids here. You know me well enough to realize I couldn't be tough on anyone.

```
Andy is describing a firefight in the
woods near Oberkaufungen where two
platoons of L Company were trapped in a
near suicide situation by the Germans.
A private, Savas J. Batsos lead not one
but two charges against the German forces
that galvanized his fellow soldiers to
leave their defensive positions and
attack. The 417th took the day but Pvt.
Batsos was killed. He was posthumously
awarded the Silver Star for his courage in
Oberkaugungen.
```

Friday, June 8, 1945

Dear Mary,

Just wrote some facts to the folks I'm doubtful about. I'm not sure Mom will take it right but I just had to tell Dad. Now that I told my folks it's past and almost forgotten. Please forgive me for breaking my promise this once. I received the June issue of Reader's Digest. It was the article on the Rhine battle that started my rambling letter home.

Letter #197 from Mary arrived today. Glad to hear the fishing equipment is on the way. I told Ernie[14] real light sinkers but I guess he figures these lakes have a tide just like the ocean. Just because I show an interest don't take this fishing business too seriously. I just want to have some fun not go into business. Bet I never even catch one fish. Golly, I can't swear at them in German.

Joe needn't fear I'll outclass him in German. I'm learning little if any. Today I was mortar range guard. I used a three word conversation to get rid of the would - be passers - by. I would say "Niene Durchgang" (no passage) and "Kanona" or cannon and illustrate an explosion with my arms. Most of the folks were satisfied and left without a word. Those that had some doubt, understood when a shell landed close. Well it is time for all little boys to be in bed. Good night and God bless you.

Love and thanks from your, Andy

---

14   Andy's Uncle Ernie Lafferty was married to his Mother's sister Olga. They lived next door to the Bergners on Rising Sun Avenue. Ernie often took Andy on overnight fishing trips to the Jersey Shore.

Saturday, June 9, 1945

Dear Mary,

Today letter #199 arrived from Ocean City. "Paddle Your Own Canoe" is a very inspiring piece of verse – completely true.

Now we are well situated in our new location in the village of Brunn near the town of Reichenbach. This is a much better set up as far as quarters go than the place we just left. I am writing this letter from the balcony that extends from my second floor room. It's nice out here tonight and no bug menace either. The yard and terrace surrounding the building is well kept by our 4 servants. The roses are now in full bloom as well as the pansies and other flowers I can't name. In a few days we will enjoy strawberries that are already turning red.

Love from your grateful, Andy

Paddle Your Own Canoe

Voyager upon life's sea,
To yourself be true,
And whatever your lot may be,
Paddle your own canoe.
Never, though the winds may rave,
Falter or look back;
But upon the darkest wave
Leave a shining track.
Paddle your own canoe.

Nobly dare the wildest storm,
Stem the hardest gale,
Brave of heart and strong of arm
You will never fail.
When the world is cold and dark,
Keep your aim in view;
And toward the beacon work,
Paddle your own canoe. ...

..Would you crush the giant wrong,
In the world's free fight?
With a spirit brave and strong,
Battle for the right.
And to break the chains that bind
The many to the few
To enfranchise slavish mind, -
Paddle your own canoe.

Nothing great is lightly won,
Nothing won is lost,
Every good deed, nobly done,
Will repay the cost.
Leave to Heaven, in humble trust,
All you will to do:
But if succeed, you must
Paddle your own canoe.

Sarah T. Bolton

Tuesday, June 12, 1945

Dear Mary,

Today I came off duty at eight o'clock a.m., ate breakfast and started out with a buddy and four chocolate bars in search of fresh eggs. Here chocolate is a magic word. Say chocolate and the eggs are yours, hens and all. We came back with 26 eier (eggs). Lately the chow hasn't been up to par that's why we will eat these eggs tonight.

Guard again from four to six and here I am. My next guard shift starts at midnight. One source of recreation for us fellows without fraulein attachments is a radio over which we hear good American songs and music. My buddy has a speaker in almost every room in the house. He can wake everybody up by just turning on the radio real loud.

You asked where we are located. I could say Werdau, Zwickau, Reichenbach or Neumarkt but that doesn't mean a thing to you. On a map we lay about 60 miles west and slightly south of Chemnitz. When the war ended we were dug in on a hill 5 kms from Chemnitz and are by degrees moving back. Well good night and God bless you.

Love from your loving, Andy

Textile Werks of Kahnes and Kohler in Werdau, Germany, converted to a Prisoner of War Camp for German Soldiers

Friday, June 15, 1945

Dear Mary,

This zone we are operating in was the disputed zone of occupation. It wasn't known whether the Russians or the Americans were to occupy here. Well now the order has placed the boundary line at the town of Zwickau[15] about 20 km's from this joint. The civils here are overjoyed that the American's will occupy instead of the Russians. "Russky nix qute." Maybe they don't think the Russian soldiers would give their gum and chocolate to the kids.

Love, Andy

Andy on occupation guard duty.

---

15   After the withdrawal of the US Army on June 30, 1945, Zwickau was occupied by the Soviet Red Army.

Sunday, June 17, 1945

Dear Mary,

Yesterday I received your letters #198, 202 & 203 and today letters #204, 205 and 206. Mary, if I ever amount to anything in life, your unsurpassed encouragement will deserve a huge share of the credit. Again, I say your letters always tie in with my problems. If something troubles me, I get the answer in your next letter. You are more to me than Mary Jane Waterman or the girl next door. You entered Burholme and that Bergner family at the exact time the Bergner family, especially the youngest Bergner boy, needed you the most. I needn't ask who sent you into my life for He is the fellow who planned all this and will give me the courage to carry it out.

So long and God bless you, Andy

Tuesday, June 19, 1945

Dear Mary,

Must tell you about my new deal. Yesterday afternoon and this afternoon I attended radio classes. I am learning to be a radio operator. There really is nothing to it. Anyone can do it if they know how and I am learning how. Today's class was very interesting because after two hours of lecture we paired up and scattered about the park with our radio sets. We used the Handy Talkie 536[16]. It weighs about 5 ½ lbs and is just what the name implies. We just gassed off about what we saw. Naturally all the fellows saw frauleins and amused us by describing them. Well I found out I wasn't very good at describing frauleins. Also found out the fellows weren't very interested in the wild ducks and carp we spotted in the lake.

Love, Andy

PRESS-TO-TALK SWITCH NOT DEPRESSED WHILE RECEIVING

Portable_radio_SCR536

---

16   The SCR - 536 was a hand - held radio transceiver used by US Signal Corps in World War II. It is popularly referred to as a walkie talkie although it was originally designated a "handie talkie."

Thursday, June 21, 1945

Dear Mary,

I must tell you that those studies I chose never materialized. Something is about to pop soon. I bet within the next two months I'll be either in the U.S.A. or the Pacific. I can always hope and maybe this short radio course will be the beginning of a break for me. There are many stories of Hitler's fate circulating. I myself have no opinion and anyway a million dollars doesn't interest me.

Your hopeful, Andy

Sunday, June 24, 1945

Dear Mary,

I am looking forward to the opportunity of criticizing your victory garden. We have a garden along the side of this house we now stay in also. An old, old man works it all day, every day and then we go eat his lettuce, strawberries and such. We now are very impatiently awaiting the arrival of the carrots. We'll have to get him to plant some radishes for I sure do like them. Are we crooks for eating the fruits of the poor old man's labor? Well anyway he seems to enjoy serving us. Yesterday he even picked a whole hatful of strawberries and gave them to us. It seems these Germans can't do enough for us. We have servants that will do anything at all you ask them to do. All you do is clap your hands twice and in about two seconds the bathtub is full of nice hot water.

About your leeks. If the bed is three square feet, it can and should be transplanted. We used to plant it in a long row and then it needn't be transplanted but we thinned it out as we used it and by the next spring we had just a few large plants. You don't need much room between the plants when you transplant them. Possibly three inches is plenty.

I'm again on the replacement list and soon will be transferred to another outfit to take some fellow's place who has 85 points. About this transfer business, the Army is discharging a number of men from here and to simplify the record keeping and paperwork, figure it simpler to fill up a whole division of 85 point men and discharge the whole works instead of working with individual men. Well our division has been chosen as the goat. All the low point men will be sent to other outfits and high point men put in this outfit. The more I try to understand, the more I know I don't know. My only hope now is to be placed in an outfit headed for the States. I'm not supposed to write about this so I can't say much more about it until it happens. Well I must go on guard again. My last shift for the day.

Love, Andy

Wednesday, June 26, 1945

Dear Mary,

Received two letters from you last night but for no reason at all was too tired to answer them. Yesterday, all day we spent on the rifle range firing transition fire with our battlefield weapons. Now that the war is over and we came out on top they want to be sure we are good shots. The entire idea was silly to me from the start. First we had to build the range and then fire. I figured why fool with death when the war is over but the big boys had different ideas.

The first day they fired on the half range there was a serious accident. As a result, five more gold stars will appear in windows back home. The war is over mind you and still men are getting killed. This isn't the only case either. If we must fire, wait until we get back to the states where they have the proper arrangements. What makes me mad, two of those fellows were to get discharges and go back to their families.

Thanks for the stationary. That really is an incentive to write. However, you'd better not send anymore with my address on it for it will change very shortly. In a way, I'll be glad to get out of this outfit.

In Joe's letter received last night I learned that one of my buddies with whom I entered service, trained and came overseas, has been wounded and is in a hospital in England. Gosh all those boys I grew up with and played ball with have been hit. It seems that way, anyway. God bless you and thanks for the Chiclets.

Love, Andy

Sunday, July 1, 1945

Dear Mary,

Two weeks before the war ended and ever since the Russians have been chasing us back towards France and today for the first time I actually gave some a good going over and talked with them. Well anyway we could both say, "ich nix versteh[17]." At first impression you'd run for the nearest hills but once you get used to the hobo appearance and very stern expressions you begin to feel your way. Then one smiled and I spotted a couple of very young looking fellows, one 21 and the other 25. That surprised me, neither looked as old as I think I do. One wore leggings and a more filthy outfit you never saw. The other, boots of a material I have never seen before. Each had a crummy looking sub - machine gun which looked as if it wouldn't even fire.

Four men relieved our platoon, four men, two bottles and a little loaf of the famous Russian bread. More men will be along later so we hear. We are still waiting to be moved southeast to Bavaria. What we will do when and if we get there no one knows. Good bye for now and God bless you.

Love, Andy

---

17 Andy's attempt at *ich verstehe nicht*, which is German for, "I don't understand."

Monday, July 2, 1945

Lauenstein

Dear Mary,

We are now at a new and better location. Andy is resting at a luxurious mountain resort[18] in the section of Germany known as Bavaria. This is very beautiful country. The only catch is, if we ever get down this mountain it'll take six weeks hard hiking to make it back up. I can quote one of my buddies, "This is the closest to God I've ever been."

How long will we be here? Ich weis nicht[19] but it won't be very long because the top brass says they will be shipping out wholesale now. What will we do here? As yet we have no chores except eating. We eat in a sunlit dining room. It reminds me of the mountain lodges in the movies, white table cloths and all. The one thing lacking to make the movie setting perfect is the absence of females. Many fellows call this a prison camp. They feel that we are being held up here away from the world because some officer wants to prove that the non - fraternization policy can be enforced. Well maybe they're in prison but I'm not. When I find the lake tomorrow I'll be all set for a good rest.

If you can't find Lauenstein on the map look for Saalfeld. It isn't too far from here. We passed there today and it was an example of U.S. precision bombing. A big armor plant was leveled and the surrounding houses unharmed. I've seen bombed areas before never such accurately devastated industrial plants. Well I am off to go exploring. Maybe I'll uncover a torture chamber or a corpse.

Love from your, Andy

---

18   Castle Lauenstein is a hilltop castle dating from the 12th Century. In the 1500 the Lords of Thyna built an elegant renaissance palace on the spot. It fell into disrepair but was restored in 1896. It is currently owned by the State of Bavaria and is operated as a museum and hotel.

19   I don't know.

Thursday, July 5, 1945

Dear Mary,

Again today the trend of the rumors are different. All shipments out of the Company have ceased momentarily and we may enjoy ourselves here for a week or two. Now I have found a spot to take a picture of the castle. This afternoon we played ball on the neighboring hill. This is a swell set-up even with the training schedule we started today but if the mail doesn't come through it can't remain a swell set-up. Golly, I've been without mail about two days and already I'm lost and moaning about it.

The weather here is fairly cold. In the morning we need jackets but in the afternoon you can pull everything off down to your undershirt. Well, I think I'll go over and get a big glass of beer so I'll sleep well tonight. I've got to go on guard from 4 to 6 in the morning.

Love from your impatient, Andy

Saturday, July 7, 1945

Dear Mary,

    Enclosed you'll find a couple post card pictures of our home. Someday next week a fellow is coming here to give us a lecture on the history of this castle. He speaks English and should be very interesting. Another hot rumor. Tomorrow a big bunch of us fellows are being shipped out. That's all the info I have maybe I'll be in the group, maybe not.

    Tonight I hiked, or rather slid, down the hill to the brewery in town and took a shower. I feel very much better now. I certainly needed it. It was my first since I've been here. We were lucky and got a hop in a jeep back up the hill. When I get some mail I'll be able to write more.

Love from your patient, Andy

Castle Lauenstein

Monday, July 9, 1945

Dear Mary,

This was a busy day for me and by the looks of things every day this week is going to be a busy day. Got up at 6:30 a.m., chow, washed up and hopped on the truck and out to the roadblock by 8:00 a.m. This unpleasant duty lasted until noon. The road block is the boundary line between the Russian and American Zones of Occupation. We have a guard post and so do the Russians. It seems the folks that satisfy us and we allow pass, the Russians refuse entry and vice versa. The reason for all the confusion is the different languages. Outside from the refusal to give in by both outposts, we get along fine and converse with one another in the little German we have and sign language. This afternoon I played ball, showered and ate twice. After I finish this letter it will be time to go on guard again. Tomorrow I have a post out in the woods so I'll be able to write more.

Love, Andy

Pfcs Zolnouski, Bergner and Cherry on the way to chow at Lauenstein Castle

Thursday, July 12, 1945

Dear Mary,

It's a different Andy writing this letter than the letters of the last couple days. Late last night we received our first mail in about 10 days. When you are accustomed to mail every day, being deprived of it for only 10 days seems an eternity. There were four letters for me and today fifteen more so I am pretty well caught up on Joe's furlough, Oxford's losing streak, the gardening, Ernie's lack of ability as a fisherman (he does miss me, at least we caught a few when I was along), Quaker activities and the BW Corp. in general.

Tomorrow more of my buddies are leaving us to join the 83rd division. From now on I'll not repeat the rumors I hear about the future. I'll bet my past letters have you thoroughly confused.

Our Russian Kamerads agree with us that Japan is tough but that they are already very decidedly beaten. Fritz's recent move has increased the tempo of the destruction being wrought on little yellow people who made such a serious blunder. Mr. Bremer's prediction can still be realized according to the views of certain military leaders. Even former Ambassador Grew now is changing his idea on the situation.

Ten more days before you folks celebrate my birthday. Nineteen. That still sounds awfully young. So far I have only one year to make up. I am very fortunate. Some fellows lost three years or more. Bye for now and all of God's choicest blessings to the W's of the BW's.

Love from your most grateful, Andy

Friday, July 13, 1945

Dear Peanut,

Today I received another letter from Buddy and he has informed me of your new nickname. He tells me you approved of it. Mary, from the sound of your letters you don't believe that Japan will crack so easy. I still have a feeling, based on nothing that this war will end just as surprisingly as it began.

Fellows are leaving the outfit thick and fast but Andy still remains. I find myself in the midst of a bunch of high point men awaiting discharge. Maybe they'll forget about me for a few months.

Your patient, waiting friend, Andy

Tuesday, July 17, 1945

Lauenstein

Dear Mary,

Now I have all the straight dope on Joe's furlough. You said maybe I'll be the next one to edge your lawn. You don't know how right you were. Don't be surprised if you see me hitch-hiking along Cottman Street while you are driving home from work. Here's the situation. Tomorrow morning at 4:45 A.M., I leave this outfit. Where am I headed? I have an idea but better not repeat it. The best answer I can give you is, "I am headed home." It may be a long drawn out journey back. My bag is packed. I haven't said anything to the folks yet. I don't want them to be disappointed if, as you say, "your plans fall through." Well good bye for now and God bless the swellest gal I know.

Love from your returning, Andy

P.S. The mail just came in. Thanks for letters # 232, 233.

Tuesday, July 31, 1945

England

Dear Mary,

It has been a very long time since I last wrote to you. At least two weeks have passed since I left the 76th Division and started the long journey back to 7427. The first lap of the trip was a four day train ride from Hof, Germany (76th Division Hdqs.) to La Harve, France. At La Harve my dreams of being home in time to celebrate Mom's birthday at home were smashed. We stayed there one whole week until last Saturday at which time we boarded the U.S. Freighter, Marine Wolf and made the short, pleasant trip to Southampton in England. A short, but long drawn out truck and train shuttle brought me here at 2:30 A.M. on my Mother's birthday. Our arrival here was a blow for we had been told that we would be transferred from Marine Wolf to the Queen Mary without setting foot on land. It wasn't until Sunday afternoon though that the boys really started to bitch. It was then we were told to prepare for a twenty day stay here at Camp Barton Stacey near Winchester, England.

This is really the best camp I have ever stayed at. The entertainment program is excellent and so are the recreational and sanitation facilities. By sanitation I mean showers. Topping all this we get leave every other day and have no chores whatsoever. With all this in mind I got prepared for my twenty days here so again this morning orders were changed and now we are supposed to leave Thursday. If so, it won't be long now.

Today I spent in the nearby English town of Andover. I had a very good time until the sun went to bed and my five buddies headed for the wine (I mean bitters), women and song. That's when I oiled up my thumb and started hitch-hiking (mostly hiking) back to camp. No hops from any Englishmen. If a G.I. truck hadn't come along I'd still be walking.

There is still hope for me to beat this letter back to the U.S.A. Well, I must write home and give the folks the good news.

Love from your USA bound, Andy

Thursday, August 2, 1945

England

Dear Mary,

Still in England but may be leaving for home any day now. Carl Grunwald is most likely now on furlough. Well you can tell him that Andy is joining his 4th Division as soon as he can get his 30 day furlough completed. Soon, I will be sweating in the heat of the sweltering sun of North Carolina. Won't it be swell, Camp Butner is only about 600 miles from home. A 3 day pass will do it. I've even figured it so I'm on furlough when the Japs give in to unconditional surrender. Think you'll be able to get me drunk then? Well good bye and God bless you.

Love from your optimistic, Andy

Sunday, August 5, 1945

England

Dear Mary,

Yes, I'm still here 3000 miles from home. No closer now than one week ago. Life here is really pleasant as far as plain living goes but we are also shut off from home and that makes it torture. If only there was a telephone here I could call you up every hour and give you the lowdown. It seems every time I drop a letter into the mail box the situation changes and again the folks back home are misinformed. At least the Army is teaching me something very new to me and that is to have patience. As things stand now we are alerted and have been for three days now and are awaiting transport home. It seems our priority rating isn't very high and we keep getting squeezed out.

Well I must be running along now you know, old chap. We G.I.s speak such good English some of the Britishers just can't understand us. Good night, God bless you and hope to see you soon.

Love from your patient, Andy

And so ended the glorious charge of the ONAWAY, the 76th Infantry Division, and their rat race through the snows and forests of Germany. From Echternach, past the Siegfried Line, through Trier, and across 20 rivers they engaged and defeated seventeen German Divisions but were never halted. The ONAWAY covered more than 400 miles in 110 continuous days of combat, capturing 33,000 prisoners and earning three battle stars. The Division was officially deactivated on August 31, 1945, at Hof, Germany. Raw replacement, 18 year old, Andy Bergner was in on 60 of those 110 days.

JUST CALL ME SOLDIER BOY

EPILOGUE

4 F   THE EVENING BULLETIN, Phila., Fri., Aug. 24, 1945

6 SHIPS DUE IN N.Y. WITH 8,693 TROOPS

One Carrying 5,135 Men Diverted from Pacific; Some from City

Six transports with 8,693 troops from Europe are scheduled to arrive in New York today, the New York Port of Embarkation has announced.

One of them, the General Breckenridge, carrying 5,135 troops, was diverted from the Pacific.

The others listed were the Fayetteville Victory, 1,865 troops; the Abraham Clark, 145; the Robin Sherwood, 634; the Reverdy Johnson, 736, and the Morris Sigman, 27.

All the arriving troops will go to Camp Kilmer, N. J.

Two other ships arrive at Boston and three at Newport News.

Units due at New York:

Aboard Abraham Clark: 666th Quartermaster Truck Company, and 314th Ordnance Bomb Disposal Squadron.

Aboard General Breckenridge; 178th Quartermaster Laundry Company, 835th Ordnance Base Depot Company; 792d, 1354th and 1358th Engineer Dump Truck Companies; Headquarters, 19th Tactical Control Group; 19th Field Medium Maintenance Squadron; 56th and 57th Signal Automatic Weapons Detachments; 16th Cavalry Reconnaissance Squadron (main body); 558th FA Battalion; 1285th and 1290th Engineer Combat Battalions; 66th Field Hospital; 33d and 36th Station Hospitals; Headquarters and Headquarters Detachment, 294th Ordnance Base Depot Company; 455th, 468th and 470th Amphibious Truck Companies; 364th Base Depot Company; 437th and 385th Port Companies, and 415th Military Police Escort Guard Company.

Aboard William N. Mulholland, 338th Station Company Squadron; 366th Financial Disbursing Section, and following units of 454th Air Service Group; 872d Air Engineer Squadron, Headquarters and Base Service Squadron, and 696th Air Materiel Squadron.

Aboard Fayetteville Victory; 15th,

15th, 19th and 26th Special Service Companies; 112th Chemical Processing Company and casual troops.

Aboard Robin Sherwood; 630th Observation Battalion; 357th Military Police Patrol Detachment, and 1792d Engineer Foundry Detachment.

Aboard Reverdy Johnson; 722d and 731st Air Materiel Squadrons, and 722d and 907th Air Engineer Squadrons.

Aboard Morris Sigman; 8275th, 8276th and 8277th Engineer Power Plant operating detachments, 262d financial disbursing section.

Arriving at Boston—Aboard Benjamin Bourne: 74 troops, surplus personnel.

Aboard James Turner: 425 troops, including 843d Air Engineer Squadron, 467th Air Materiel Squadron, miscellaneous air force personnel, personnel for reassignment and duty, personnel for discharge and medical attendants.

At Newport News

At Newport News, Va.:

Aboard West Point: 7,728 troops, including these elements of 85th Infantry Division; Headquarters and Headquarters Company, band, medical detachment and special troops, Military Police Platoon, 785th Ordnance Company; 85th Quartermaster Company; 85th Signal Company, 338th and 339th Infantries, Headquarters and Headquarters Battery, 85th Division Artillery; 328th, 329th, 403d and 910 Field Artillery Battalions; 310th Engineer Battalion, 310th Medical Battalion and 85th Cavalry Reconnaissance Troops.

Aboard J. K. Jones: Ten troops, undesignated units.

Aboard Lake C. Victory: 1,940 troops, mostly Negro, undesignated units. Aboard George H. Dern: 742 troops, undesignated units.

Men on board the S. S. Buxton Gwynett due at Boston, are:

Yeaer, Cpl. John, 317 W. Chew av.
Altman, T/5 Harold, 3219 S. 17th st.
Calazzis, T/4 Joseph, 2942 E. Franklin st.
Barden, Pfc. Joseph, 3621 E. Marlon st.
Mehl, T/5 John J., 2251 Gerritt st.
Petillo, Pfc. J., 3000 Disston st.
Schaefer, Pfc. F., 231 E. Chelten lane.
Shearer, Pfc. F., 7129 W. Cambridge st.
Staskiewics, Pfc. J., 2331 S. Titus av.
Stevenson, Pfc. D., 4403 Larchwood av.
Vaulhorn, S., 2341 Maiden drive.
Bach, Pfc. F., 2327 Friendship st.
Balich, Pfc. M., 3653 W. Gordon st.
Bergner, Pfc. Andrew, 3427 Elsing Sum av.
Blick, Pfc. W., 3914 Chestnut st.
Barden, Pfc. M., 622 French st.
Brindisi, Pfc. N., 128 N. Queen lane.
Caben, Pfc. Arthur, 4621 N. 9th st.
DeNardo, Pfc. A., 537 Reeve st.
Ferrara, Pfc. Thomas, 444 E. 31th st.
Godshall, Pfc. Robert, 302 E. Highland av.
Hatch, Pfc. Leo, 4256 Ternhill road.

Newspapers across America published lists of returning troop ships along with the names and addresses of local soldiers lucky enough to come home. The Philadelphia Evening Bulletin of Friday, August 24, noted that six ships carrying local men were due into New York harbor; two more would dock in Boston and three in Newport News, Virginia. In total they carried more than 20,000 troops. Some of these ships had been headed for the Pacific war but were diverted after the Japanese surrender. Aboard the Lake C. Victory, scheduled to dock in Newport News, were 1,940 troops, mostly Negro. Even in transportation, the military was segregated during World War II. Sailing from Southampton on the S.S. Button Gwynett, Private Bergner docked in Boston on August 24, 1945, almost six months from the day he left for Europe and war.

Fred "Pop - Pop" Bergner, leading the band.

There is no record of the reunion party that welcomed Andy back to Burholme or even when he finally arrived home. But in an ironic twist, the welcome home party most assuredly included a keg of stout beer, wieners and sauerkraut, Pop Pop Bergner wearing his Tyrolean hat and leading the oompa band. All the characters mentioned in Andy's letters home would have been spilling out of the house and onto the lawn at 7427 Rising Sun Ave, unselfconsciously celebrating their German heritage. Even from a distance of almost 60 years, it is not hard to imagine the joy and thanksgiving my grandparents felt as they saw all three of their sons, Fritz, Joe and Andy, home and safe and whole.

But, as a "low point man" Andy's tour of duty was not over and on October 15, 1945, his furlough at an end, he began a period of stateside service that would include assignments at Camp Butner in Raleigh, North Carolina, and Fort McClellan in Anniston, Alabama. During this period Andy wrote to Mary nearly every day describing camp life, frustration at not being promoted, his thoughts about future careers, political commentary on the newly formed United Nations Organization and labor strikes, movies, college football and always counting down the days until he was released from service and could return to civilian life.

"This Army life is a vacation before hard work. This is the first vacation I ever wanted to end."

Apparently, Andy's duties at Camp Butner were light. Mornings were spent in weapons training, mapping or other education classes with physical activity in the afternoon. Occasionally he pulled "CQ" (change of quarters) duty which involved answering phones and delivering messages at headquarters. He drove officers around the base in a jeep, was trained to drive 1.5 - ton trucks and of course, there was the inevitable

The reunited Bergner family in 1945. Back – Kate, Fred, Ida and Madge. Front – Fritz, Blanche, Joe and Andy.

KP duty. At first Andy described his stint at Camp Butner as a vacation after the rigors of Germany, but inactivity was not part of his DNA and he began to feel as if he was just marking time. While he generally approached life cheerfully, flashes of frustration occasionally seeped through the letters. "If only I could get a position that would keep me busy like I want to be. I can't dispense the feeling that any day in the service is a day wasted.

Andy (right) showing off his jeep at Ft. Buchner.

First it's important to become interested in my work and that's tough for there's no responsibility at all."

He was frustrated at not being promoted to corporal, complaining to Mary Jane:

"I just don't agree with the way Lt. Clark does things. Maybe I'm just mad because he hasn't as yet given me one of the ratings he could. Maybe I'm at fault and don't deserve it but at any rate I'm still a P.F.C."

He also chafed at being required to learn to fire a new automatic carbine, saying, "I wish I'd never had to fire any weapon again, but this is still the Army, for the next few months anyway." After leaving the service, Andy never did fire another gun.

If life on base was dull, Andy took full advantage of the proximity to Raleigh Durham. He and his buddies attended college football games at North Carolina State and Duke where servicemen got in for 50 cents if they would sit in the visiting team's section. They paid a $1.25 to watch Ben Hogan and Sam Snead play golf in the Durham Open at Hope Valley Country Club and heard Benny Goodman jam at the sports arena. Bowling was 10 cents a lane. An excellent meal at the Service Club "was worth every bit of the 90 cents."

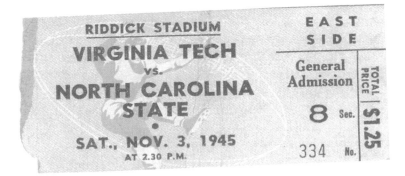

Movies were inexpensive and **Andy saw many** - "City of Conquest" with James Cagney; "The Green Years"; "Night and Day" based on the life of Cole Porter; "The Road to Utopia" with Bob and Bing. But his favorite was "The Bells of St. Mary's" starring Bing Crosby and Ingrid Bergman. Andy compared Sister Benedict's faith that worked a miracle in the movie to his faith that pulled him through the war.

He also writes a lot about listening to the radio that Mary Jane sent him, Lionel Barrymore and Margret O'Brien on the Lux Soap Radio Program, Blondie and The Grand Ole Oprie, which Andy described as "the hillbilly music that they so love here." He played on the Camp baseball team and became quite a pool shark, once winning $14. And topping the list of entertainments was the rare but coveted three-day pass - just enough time to take a train to Burholme and see his family for a day and night before making the return trip.

Andy and Mary often discussed politics. Andy was a supporter of efforts to establish the United Nations Organization, "UNO", though in March 1946 he wrote, "If people would wise up and pattern their lives as the Divine Architect wants them to, there would be no need for the UNO or UNRRA[1]". A nationwide rail strike in May of the same year caused the cancelation of a long awaited furlough and prompted Andy to write:

"As soon as the rail strike went into effect all furloughs were canceled. I guess I should sit down and sulk but what good would that do. I admire Mr. Truman for the way he flared

1   United Nations Relief and Rehabilitation Administration

up and frightened the railroad workers back on the job but I'm afraid I'm not entirely in agreement with his Strike Draft Policy. You must know that to force a man to do a certain job isn't democracy its socialism. On the other hand, to demand that the management always make concessions for labor would be a form of communism. The middle path of freedom can only be maintained by making both management and labor work together for each other's good. Capital should give the workers a small percentage of excess profit as a bonus for a job well done. Labor should be made to realize the justifiable profits of capital and respect the property of the firms they are employed by…Instead of bucking heads, these two backbones of the nation should work for the common good."

However, overarching all of the descriptions of camp life and entertainments was concern for the future. Andy's father Fredrick Bergner, who had no formal education beyond eighth grade, was determined that all three of his sons would go to Villanova College[2] and graduate with degrees in mechanical engineering. Andy was interested in chemistry and spent hours in the camp library reading, "Your Career in Chemistry" and "So You Want to be a Chemist". He practiced chemistry and math problems and talked of visiting the Dupont plant in Fayetteville to see practical applications of chemistry.

Also, during this time Andy seriously contemplated a calling to be a priest. He believed then and still believes today that he had been saved by divine intervention many times during the short but brutal weeks in Germany. He felt he owed God his life and should give that life back to the church. He discussed this calling with his brother Joe, his Dad, and his cousin Bill Seelaus, who had recently been ordained and of course he sought counsel from his best friend, Mary Jane. Throughout his life Andy never lost that deep spirituality but eventually decided that he didn't need to be a priest to preach the gospel, as he explained to Mary, "Preaching hardly ever reaches the ears of people who need it but a good example always hits the jackpot."

---

2   Villanova was founded by Augustinian Friars in 1841 and after a couple temporary closures has been operating continuously since 1865. The college is located 12 miles west of Philadelphia and until 1853 was an all male school. Villanova achieved university status in 1953 at which time it also began admitting female students.

Before Andy could implement any career plans he needed to get out of the Army and that was not as easy as he wished. At one point he suggested jokingly to Mary, "Maybe if you folks refused to pay taxes or buy war bonds, Uncle would have to give me those walking papers." In January 1946 enlisted men were divided into three categories based on the number of service points they had acquired. Men with less than 36 points were eligible to be re - deployed overseas; Andy was in this group. In an uncharacteristic expression of rebellion, Andy wrote,

> "Maybe we unfortunates who got enough war to make us appreciate life, but not enough to be eligible for discharge would be better off to refuse to serve Uncle further in foreign lands and sweat our time out in the stockade. We are seriously considering what action to take if they make any drastic moves around here. If they sent us over the pond again we would really be bad off. I suppose Congress figures we can't vote so they don't give a damn about us."
>
> Love from your hurting, Andy"

Throughout January and February rumors about re - deployments flew around camp. Finally, the word came, not from the brass but from the *Durham Sun* newspaper, that the Fourth Infantry would be inactivated and all the boys at Camp Butner transferred to either the 16th or Third Mechanized Cavalry. But where? Anxiety about oversees postings mounted until March 3 when Andy learned he was being sent further south, to Fort McClellan, Alabama. Too far for a three-day pass home, but a continent away from the occupation army in Europe. It was good enough for this soldier.

CO. D, 10TH TRAINING BATTALION
I.R.T.C.
FORT MCCLELLAN, ALABAMA

Saturday Mar. 30, 1946

#395

Dear Mary
Oh what a beautiful morning Oh a

For a boy from Philadelphia, Fort McClellan, surrounded as it was by mountains and nearly 50,000 acres of National Forest, was truly the middle of nowhere. The camp itself was huge, able to house 50,000 troops and encompassing 74 miles of roads, a hospital with 80 buildings, five theaters, an amphitheater that seated 12,000 and hundreds of 15-man huts to house recruits. McClellan was one of the largest Infantry Replacement Training Centers in the country. Andy, now 19 and a battle veteran, became a cadreman training recent draftees. From the outset, softhearted Andy didn't think this assignment was going to work.

March 6, 1946

"I am to be a Cadreman, training the newly drafted eighteen year olds. It's really a shame the way these lads are treated by some sergeants who have no feelings and make no allowances for the ignorance of their charges. Don't expect me to get any rating[3] for bullying a bunch of kids. I'm not that type."

And two days later:

"Today I got my first real taste of training rookies. Ninety eight of these lads joined our company today and Andy was required to take an active part in getting them equipped and straightened out. My, what questions they can ask. This afternoon I marched twenty - five of them to the barber shop. During the forty - five minutes I waited with them they must have fired a couple hundred questions at me. My impression is that most of them are scared inside but try to be bold.

---

3 Promotion

The majority look so small it seems impossible they are of age. We, the Cadre, have been instructed to treat them rough as inferiors. That's the way I was treated anyway. It seemed wrong to me then and still does."

Then on March 9, only three days into his new training career, Andy was reading in the day room when the Mess Sergeant came in complaining that he was short two cooks. Within the hour, Andy, who had never cooked over anything except a scout campfire, consented to cook for the company. He was one of four cooks working under the direction of the Mess Sergeant. In teams of two they worked 24 hours on and 24 hours off preparing breakfast, lunch, dinner and sometimes late night snacks for 169 men. Though he said the hours were "queer" and he had trouble adjusting to only a few hours of sleep one night and many, many hours the next, Andy seemed to really take to the work. On March 13, after only three days on the job he wrote:

"Those hours I watched Mom when I was a kid are coming in handy. No more of that uncooked tasteless sauerkraut in our mess hall. Yesterday I took care that it was fully cooked and I dropped a few onions and apple and salt and pepper in and the fellows couldn't eat enough of it. It gives you a feeling of pride to be able to satisfy the boys."

By the end of March Andy was able to answer Mary Jane's questions about the camp kitchen.

"We have a routine master menu for the month. From this the Mess Sergeant makes up his meals, usually not following it [master menu] very closely. We follow the Sgt's menu fairly close. Of course if we think the meal would be better tasting with French fried spuds instead of mashed we are permitted to do as we see fit. The rations are delivered daily and we have no say in what is sent but when we get it, we prepare it as we choose. Ability in cooking is not about knowing a lot of recipes, its knowing what will be a good combination. Seasoning is the best trick for tasty food."

Andy writes about cutting up 500 pork chops and deciding he does not want to be a butcher, about creatively re-using leftovers that the other cooks would have thrown away and about staying up late to bake cakes.

"It's 9:30 P.M. and the mess hall will be buzzing for a couple of hours yet. The boys are on a two hour night problem and we're to have hot coffee and cake for their refresher and before bed snack. I don't mind this extra work because I realize what it means to come in wet and tired and get a cup of hot coffee. The boys really need it and appreciate it in spite of all the grumbling about only getting one piece of cake. What we feed is good food but no matter how hard we try we can't get enough to fill some of these lads. Well, they are all gaining weight, no malnutrition cases yet so I guess we can rest at ease."

On April 18, 1946, the Thursday before Easter, Andy wrote, "I must work this entire weekend. Even working on Easter Sunday isn't too bad. Last Easter Sunday we were fighting. Last Good Friday many of my buddies died. Last Holy Thursday, most of the boys fell into German hands. Hey, that seems to fit in with that first Holy Week many years ago."

The hard and fulfilling work in the kitchens at Fort McClellan certainly proved a benefit to Andy when he became a husband and then father of five hungry children. His beautiful wife Audrey, who came to the marriage with only a working knowledge of toll house cookies, eventually learned to cook but never especially cared for it. It was Andy who could set up a production line to pack 25 school lunch bags on Sunday night, freezing twenty to be pulled out of the freezer, five at a time, on Tuesday, Wednesday, etc. It was Andy who could flip pancakes for 300 at the Shove Tuesday Church Supper. It was Andy who took every item of food in the refrigerator and put it in a pot with the turkey carcass for a hearty soup that lasted several days. As he would say, it's all in the seasoning.

While the work made the months at Fort McClellan go faster, he was still far away from home. In May 1946 he wrote to Mary, "Dark clouds are drifting over my hopes of an early discharge. All I ask is that I become a civilian before the month of August starts." During this period of waiting, letters from his family and especially from Mary Jane were like life's blood. In all, between September 1944 and July 1946, Mary Jane Waterman wrote 473 numbered letters to Andy Bergner and sent countless packages including gifts of food, clothing, appliances, envelopes addressed not only to herself but to Andy's many other friends,

magazine subscriptions, poems and for the entire stateside tour of
duty a weekly shipment of peanuts in the shell was delivered to
Andy every Thursday. All of Andy's buddies came to know and
love "MJ" through her letters and generous gifts of food.
A May 1946 letter to Andy from his best buddy John Fliss
captures the impact that she had on all the guys.

> "Good old M.J. There is no need in my asking if the
> peanuts, pennies and literature are coming regularly for
> its undoubtedly so. You know Andy, I'm amazed at how
> considerate, unselfish and generous she is. A person like her
> should deserve the best of everything in the world. I don't
> believe in these Lonely Hearts Club romances, but she is
> truly one girl any fellow could fall in love with through
> correspondence, which is in accord with the statement that
> beauty is only skin deep."

In letter after letter, signed, Love from your grateful Andy;
Love from your true Andy; Love from your tired Andy; Love
from your smiley Andy; Love from your Soldier Boy, he tells Mary
Jane how important she is to him. On October 30, 1945, shortly
after arriving at Camp Butner, he wrote,

> "I'm the luckiest fellow alive to have such a friend as good
> and faithful as you are Mary. You may or may not quite
> realize what your faithfulness means to me or has done for
> me in the past. I have just passed
> through one of the most trying
> and dangerous periods of life
> and your letters, kindness and
> most of all your never ceasing
> encouragement enabled me to
> stay alert and withstand the
> slings and arrows of outrageous
> fortune. With God's help I hope
> never to disappoint you or break
> the trust you must have in me."

The love between Andy and Mary Jane was an intense and
highly personal friendship uncomplicated by sex or romance. It
may have started as Mary Jane's civic duty – her war effort – but
the crinkled pages in the blue notebook tell a story of affection
between an 18-year-old boy and a 35-year-old woman that defied
conventional norms.

ENLISTED RECORD AND REPORT OF SEPARATION
HONORABLE DISCHARGE

1. LAST NAME — FIRST NAME — MIDDLE INITIAL	2. ARMY SERIAL NO.	3. SEC. — 5	4. ARM OR SERVICE	5. COMPONENT
BERGNER ANDREW L	33 952 189	21 MAY 46	INF	AUS
6. ORGANIZATION		7. DATE OF SEPARATION	8. PLACE OF SEPARATION	SEPARATION CENTER
CO L 417TH INF REG 76TH DIV		12 JUL 46	FT GEO G MEADE MD	
9. PERMANENT ADDRESS FOR MAILING PURPOSES		10. DATE OF BIRTH	11. PLACE OF BIRTH	
7427 RISING SUN AVE PHILADELPHIA PA		22 JUL 26	PHILADELPHIA PA	
12. ADDRESS FROM WHICH EMPLOYMENT WILL BE SOUGHT		13. COLOR EYES	14. COLOR HAIR	15. HEIGHT	16. WEIGHT	17. NO. DEPEND.
SEE 9		BLUE	BROWN	6'	185 LBS	0
18. RACE	19. MARITAL STATUS	20. U.S. CITIZEN	21. CIVILIAN OCCUPATION AND NO.
WHITE X	SINGLE X	YES X	STUDENT HIGH SCH SCIENTIFIC X-02

MILITARY HISTORY

22. DATE OF INDUCTION	23. DATE OF ENLISTMENT	24. DATE OF ENTRY INTO ACTIVE SERVICE	25. PLACE OF ENTRY INTO SERVICE
29 SEP 44		29 SEP 44	PHILADELPHIA PA

SELECTIVE SERVICE	26. REGISTERED	27. LOCAL S.S. BOARD NO.	28. COUNTY AND STATE	29. HOME ADDRESS AT TIME OF ENTRY INTO SERVICE
X	#85		PHILADELPHIA PA	SEE 9

30. MILITARY OCCUPATIONAL SPECIALTY AND NO.	31. MILITARY QUALIFICATION AND DATE (i.e., Infantry, Aviation and marksmanship badges, etc.)
TRUCK DRIVER LIGHT 345	COMBAT INF BADGE SS M1 RIFLE EXP LMG

32. BATTLES AND CAMPAIGNS
GO33WD45 RHINELAND CENTRAL EUROPE

33. DECORATIONS AND CITATIONS
ARMY OCCUPATION MEDAL (GERMANY) GOOD CONDUCT MEDAL AMERICAN THEATER RIBBON EUROPEAN-AFRICAN-MIDDLE EASTERN THEATER RIBBON WORLD WAR II VICTORY RIBBON

34. WOUNDS RECEIVED IN ACTION
NONE

35. LATEST IMMUNIZATION DATES				36. SERVICE OUTSIDE CONTINENTAL U.S. AND RETURN			
SMALLPOX	TYPHOID	TETANUS	OTHER (specify)	DATE OF DEPARTURE	DESTINATION	DATE OF ARRIVAL
OCT 44	OCT 44	APR 45	TYP FEB 45	24 FEB 45	SCOTLAND	3 MAR 45
				10 AUG 45	#3329338 UNITED STATES	23 AUG 45

37. TOTAL LENGTH OF SERVICE				38. HIGHEST GRADE HELD
CONTINENTAL SERVICE		FOREIGN SERVICE		TEC-5
YEARS	MONTHS	DAYS	YEARS	MONTHS	DAYS
1	3	17	0	6	0

39. PRIOR SERVICE
NONE

40. REASON AND AUTHORITY FOR SEPARATION
AR 615-365 DTD 15 DEC 44 RR 1-1 & PAR 1B CIR 163 HQS 2ND ARMY DTD 2 JUL 46

41. SERVICE SCHOOLS ATTENDED		42. EDUCATION (Years)
NONE		Grammar 8	High School 4	College 0

PAY DATA   VOUCHER #1156

43. LONGEVITY FOR PAY PURPOSES		44. MUSTERING OUT PAY		45. SOLDIER DEPOSITS	46. TRAVEL PAY	47. TOTAL AMOUNT, NAME OF DISBURSING OFFICER	
YEARS	MONTHS	DAYS	TOTAL	THIS PAYMENT	NONE	$5.75	$349.35	PEARSON MAJOR FD
	9	14	300.00	100.00				

INSURANCE NOTICE

IMPORTANT IF PREMIUM IS NOT PAID WHEN DUE OR WITHIN THIRTY-ONE DAYS THEREAFTER, INSURANCE WILL LAPSE. MAKE CHECKS OR MONEY ORDERS PAYABLE TO THE TREASURER OF THE U.S. AND FORWARD TO COLLECTIONS SUBDIVISION, VETERANS ADMINISTRATION, WASHINGTON 25, D.C.

48. KIND OF INSURANCE		49. HOW PAID	50. Effective Date of Allotment Discontinuance	51. Date of Next Premium Due	52. PREMIUM DUE	53. INTENTION OF VETERAN TO
Nat. Serv.	U.S. Govt.	None	Allotment	Direct to V.A.				Continue	Discontinue
X				X	31 JUL 46	31 AUG 46	$ 6.40	X	

54. REMARKS (This space for completion of above items or entry of other items specified in W.D. Directives)
LAPEL BUTTON ISSUED NO TIME LOST UNDER AW 107 ASR SCORE 27

55. SIGNATURE OF PERSON BEING SEPARATED	56. PERSONNEL OFFICER (Type name, grade and organization — signature)
Andrew L. Bergner	G D HINES 2D LT CE

WD AGO FORM 53-55
1 November 1944
This form supersedes all previous editions of WD AGO Forms 53 and 55 for enlisted persons entitled to an Honorable Discharge, which will not be used after receipt of this revision.

-165-

On August 31, 1946, Andy received an honorable discharge from the U.S. Army and returned to Burholme in time to register for the fall semester at Villanova College. Though the letters and peanut deliveries stopped after Andy returned home, the "BW Corporation" lasted many more years. In 1947 Mary Jane gave Andy the greatest gift of his life by introducing him to the girl who would become his cherished bride of 58 years.

Quite the matchmaker, MJ was also responsible for brother Joe meeting his bride. When Joe agreed to tend bar at a wedding shower Mary was giving he was smitten by beautiful Edith Dodszuweit. They married in 1950 immediately after his graduation from Villanova with a degree in - of course - mechanical engineering.

Andy with fiancée Audrey Bodine at his graduation from Villanova on June 2, 1951. They were married seven days later.

In 1951, Mary Jane danced at Andy's wedding to Audrey Windsor Bodine. When the newlyweds moved to New York and eventually Virginia, Pennsylvania, California, Florida and Arizona, the unusual love story between Private First Class Andy Bergner and Mary Jane Waterman became a memory captured only in the letters, pictures and mementos so carefully preserved in the blue notebook.

My Dad never talked to his children about the war but throughout his life he modeled a patriotism based on respect and responsibility for this country. The words he used on November 8, 1945, to describe his feelings about America are still true for him today.

Dear Mary Jane,

"This afternoon we had a retreat parade at post
headquarters. It's something like that that makes you glad
you're in the service. Everyone is standing at attention
saluting in the direction of the slowly retreating flag. As the
Old Glory falters down the rope, the band is planning the
Star Spangled Banner. You look that flag square in the eye
and you say, "Buddy, I have a share in you."

Then your thoughts carry you to the woods near
Obergefungen, the towns of Schmitten and Dorfweil and
other places where you saw your buddies fall and die for that
flag you now salute. A quick silent prayer goes up for those
men as that flag comes down. Months, and for some fellows
years of hardship are relived in those few seconds. Yes I did
my share. Maybe not as much as some others, maybe much
more but at any rate I can say, "I did my share". Maybe this
sounds patriotic or silly. Maybe its propaganda but the feeling
is there and every fellow on that field who can face that flag
feels the same way.

Yes, this is still the best country on earth. Sure many
things are yet to be corrected but that's our job and we
all have the opportunity to adjust this country to suit the
majority. Well, good night and God bless you.

Your grateful, loving friend, Andy

P.S. The peanuts arrived today at noon and are already
consumed. The fellows want to know if you live on a peanut
plantation."

ANDREW L. BERGNER

To you who answered the call of your country and served in its Armed Forces to bring about the total defeat of the enemy, I extend the heartfelt thanks of a grateful Nation. As one of the Nation's finest, you undertook the most severe task one can be called upon to perform. Because you demonstrated the fortitude, resourcefulness and calm judgment necessary to carry out that task, we now look to you for leadership and example in further exalting our country in peace.

Harry Truman

THE WHITE HOUSE

POST SCRIPT

While researching to provide context to this collection of letters, I learned that through the National Archives that military personnel can obtain replacement medals for those that they earned in service but may have been lost over time. I thought it would be nice to get my father's medals and frame them for him as a memento. I completed the online request and waited only a short time for the package to arrive. Included in with the sharp shooter medallions, combat infantry badge, good conduct award, campaign ribbons for Europe and the German Occupation and the World War II Victory Medal, was a Bronze Star for Valor with my father's name inscribed on the back. Just another part of his war experience that Private Bergner never talked about.

Laurie Bergner Maggiano

Bronze Star

Andy, Fritz and Joe home on leave

Bergner Family Before the War - Back Row - Andy, Joe,
Madge and Freddie - Front Row Catherine, Fred and Ida